MAKE
BIG
PROFITS
ON
eBay

MAKE BIG PROFITS ON eBay

Start Your Own Million $ Business

JACQUELYN LYNN AND CHARLENE DAVIS

EP
Entrepreneur.
Press

Managing editor: Jere L. Calmes
Cover design: Pay Fan
Composition and production: Eliot House Productions

This publication is designed to provide accurate and authoritative information in regard to the subject matter covered. It is sold with the understanding that the publisher is not engaged in rendering legal, accounting, or other professional services. If legal advice or other expert assistance is required, the services of a competent professional person should be sought.

Library of Congress Cataloging-in-Publication Data is available

ISBN 1-932531-27-0

Printed in Canada

11 10 09 08 07 06 05   10 9 8 7 6 5 4 3 2 1

Table of Contents

CHAPTER 3

Getting Set Up as an eBay Seller 25

CHAPTER 6

The Tools of Your eBay Trade 67

CHAPTER 7

Great Listings Are the Foundation of Selling on eBay 75

CHAPTER 12

Add Revenue with eBay Subsidiaries 149

CHAPTER 13

Make Money on eBay without Selling Anything 155

CHAPTER 14

Fundraising on eBay 161

Acknowledgments

A BOOK WRITTEN FOR AND ABOUT A community of millions of people around the globe is never a solo project. We would like to thank the following eBay sellers who were so generous with their time and advice: Liz Baker (theliteratelady), Bob Bidwell (plates-n-stuff), Cynthia Bull (Elance ID: cynrje), Maggie Donapel (plumsbooks), Jonathan Garriss (gothamcityonline), Rhonda Haney (7713November), Georgene Harkness (mynewthreads), Gary Hunt (speedwind), Michael Jansma (gemaffair), Fred Johnson (quikdropflcas), Karen Kelley (thepinkboutique), Kathy Logan (rosie_peachstate), Steve Mack (ztradingpost), Gary Neubert (gatorpack), Jim Salvas (camerajim), Seth Schmidt (shutterbladestore), Lisa Singer (highend0), Randy Smythe (glacierbaydvd), Nona Van Deusen (stylebug.com), Ron and Sheri Walker (beansantiques), and David Wombacher (camerahunter).

In addition to the eBay users we've named, we'd like to thank all the buyers and sellers we've done business with over the years who have contributed to our understanding and knowledge of this incredible marketplace.

Most importantly, we thank the folks at eBay, from founder Pierre Omidyar to Meg Whitman, president and CEO, and everyone in between who have worked so hard to create this opportunity—for the users, and for us.

Preface

BOUGHT IT ON EBAY.

I sold it on eBay.

These phrases were not part of our vocabulary just a decade ago. But now, treasures are found every day on eBay, and an increasing number of multimillion-dollar businesses are serving their customers through this intriguing venue.

Want to be part of the excitement?

Better yet, want to use eBay to build your own business?

You've come to the right place. Join us as we explore the many ways you can profit with eBay.

—*Jacquelyn Lynn and Charlene Davis*

For Jerry and Joe
They know why.

CHAPTER 1

The Wonderful World of eBay

O F ALL THE TECHNOLOGICAL ADVANCES that have changed the way businesses operate, the internet is arguably the one with the greatest impact. E-commerce has found a clear and permanent place in the business world. And under that huge umbrella of "doing business on the internet" falls a legendary business success story: eBay.

eBay began as a simple little web site created to provide buyers and sellers a cyber-place where they could trade directly with one another. Pierre Omidyar launched AuctionWeb—eBay Internet in 1995. A year later, the site had nearly 10,000 users, and the following year, passed the one million mark in items sold.

In 1998, the company went public, and by 2000, the gross merchandise sales on eBay topped $1 billion. Today, there are more than 115 million registered eBay users (more than 48 million are active), annual gross merchandise sales exceed $8 billion (about a quarter of that is from business purchases), the company is operating globally, and nearly half a million people are supporting their families with businesses that sell on eBay.

These are just a few of the remarkable statistics about eBay. But what do these numbers mean for you? They mean an extraordinary opportunity to reach a worldwide market with your product, whatever that happens to be.

Consider this: About 8 million people live in New York City; fewer than 3.75 million in Los Angeles; about 2 million in Houston; and just under 400,000 in Omaha. If you were to open a retail store in any of those cities, do you think your market would be even 1 percent of the overall population?

eBay has expanded any retail seller's market from a relatively small local group to essentially anyone with a computer and access to the internet. Major companies, both business-to-consumer and business-to-business, have realized that this is a sales opportunity they can't afford to overlook. For the start-up operation and even existing small business owners who sell on eBay, this means they've stepped on a level playing field. Your chances of profits and success are just as good as a part-time seller who posts a couple of auctions a month or the huge multinational corporation with thousands of items up for sale at any given time.

Successful eBay sellers come from all backgrounds and have an infinite range of experience and goals. Their products range from vehicles to sporting goods to jewelry to business equipment to just about anything you can think of. We even found a mother of three young children offering what was left of her sanity for sale.

Here's what the high-dollar eBay sellers have in common:

- *They treat their eBay operation like a business.* This means creating a business entity with a name, bank account, proper licenses, identifiable legal structure, and whatever else is appropriate for a particular operation. It also means finding reliable suppliers and building solid relationships with them. And it means providing superior customer service, shipping promptly, and leaving timely, accurate feedback.

- *They invest in their business.* They have adequate computers and printers, high-speed internet service, and digital cameras. They properly equip their business with the essentials for shipping (work tables, scales, packing tools, etc.); and they are willing to spend money on software and services to enhance their operation.

- *They find a niche and build on their expertise.* Yes, you can sell just about anything on eBay, but it's impossible for any one person to be an expert in all the categories of merchandise on eBay. Successful eBay sellers choose one or two product lines and become experts in those areas. Sellers who deal in collectibles and unique items supplement their own knowledge by building a reference library. "I probably own 1,000 books [about vintage toys]," says Gary Hunt (eBay User ID: speedwind), who started selling old toys on eBay after taking early retirement from the corporate world. Hunt's vintage toy sales exceed $500,000 a year; he gets higher prices for his items because he knows what he's doing and that knowledge is clear to his customers when they read his descriptions.

- *They understand the value of great communication.* Successful eBay sellers know how to write auction listings that accurately and completely describe the product, shipping, payment options, return policy, and other essentials. They respond to questions from bidders promptly, with complete and courteous answers. They communicate with winning bidders immediately at the close of the auction and maintain that communication until the transaction is complete. "You can't just respond to an e-mail two days later or ship a week later," says Nona Van Deusen (eBay User ID: stylebug.com), who sells high-end designer clothing. When her customers ask a question about a garment or sizing, they want an answer fast—and if they don't get it, they probably won't bid on the item. But when they're happy with the service, they'll buy from her again.

- *They are persistent and learn by doing.* Successful eBay sellers don't give up easily. When an auction doesn't go as expected, they figure out what to do differently the next time for better results. They learn from their mistakes— and from what they do well.

- *They are creative and always open to new ideas.* "You can't think traditionally when you're doing eBay," says Randy Smythe (eBay User ID: glacierbaydvd) in Anaheim, California. He says if you're not good at thinking outside the box, you aren't likely to do well on eBay.

- *They love what they do.* Buying and selling on eBay is fun, and that makes it easy to work hard at it. "That's why they are so successful, because it's a lot of fun," says Steve Mack (eBay User ID: ztradingpost). "They are passionate about it; they love it."

What Can You Sell on eBay?

The short answer to that question is "just about anything." eBay does have some restrictions based on legal and safety issues, but most legitimate products can be sold on the site. That means if you want to start a new business selling on eBay, the issue you'll most need to be concerned with is finding a product that you'll enjoy working with.

If you already have a business, use eBay as an additional selling platform. The cost is minimal, and more than one retailer has ended up closing their brick-and-mortar store in favor of operating more profitably on eBay.

High-end clothiers use eBay to move their designer items that didn't sell in the store. Crafters use eBay to supplement their show sales—or as a more comfortable alternative to working the arts-and-crafts show circuit. Consignment stores and pawn shops have found eBay a great way to reach more potential customers. Restaurants sell their signature items, such as salad dressings and sauces, on eBay. Some retailers will auction the same sale items that are being sold simultaneously in their stores, because they realize what a huge audience they have on eBay. Even educational courses—home study courses on real estate, business, languages, mathematics, hypnosis, sports, and more—are auctioned on eBay. Sellers of all kinds of products use eBay as a means to reach a worldwide market.

eBay also works as a way to test-market products and price points for other retail channels. For example, if you have a new product—one you've developed yourself or one you've just discovered—use eBay to identify your market and determine the most effective pricing. Invest a few months of test-selling on eBay, then use the information you gather in the process to fine-tune your business plan.

Although almost anything goes on eBay, there are some prohibited items such as livestock, prescription drugs, firearms, and child pornography. Body parts are also banned from being sold on eBay. A few years ago, an auction for a live kidney reached $5,750,100 before eBay yanked it. Someone even tried to sell her virginity, but eBay immediately canceled the listing before anyone could find out what it was worth.

Though these examples make for amusing conversation, the bottom line is this: If you're serious about starting your own business and you want to sell on eBay, you can find something you enjoy working with that will allow you to make plenty of money. You can do it exclusively on eBay, or you can blend your eBay efforts with other sales channels. Van Deusen, for example, started out selling exclusively on eBay, then created her own web site, then opened a retail store. Currently, about 30 percent of her total sales are through eBay.

THE SEASONS OF eBAY

Most retailers experience seasonal volume fluctuations, and eBay sellers are no different. Certainly there will always be exceptions, but in general, eBay sales pick up in January and February, begin to slow in March, often stay slow through the summer months, then pick up after Labor Day and stay strong until mid-December.

Not the Only Game in Town

Online auctions are a $2.5 billion-plus industry. There are hundreds of sites operating around the world. Some specialize and restrict listings to a particular category, such as art, automobiles, books, electronics, memorabilia, business services, and travel. General auction sites offer a wide variety of categories and compete for sellers on service and price.

There is absolutely no reason why you can't sell on more than one auction site; just don't list the same item on two or more sites at the same time. There are good reasons to diversify. You may find that used books will sell easier at Amazon.com, but if you have some that aren't moving, you could relist them at Half.com or Yahoo! Of course, if your "used book" is a rare, inscribed, first edition, you may want to auction it on eBay or even a specialty site to get more and potentially higher bids.

Before you start selling products on any online auction site, be sure to read its terms and conditions first. Each one has different policies and procedures and you will want to become familiar with those whose auction sites you participate on. Here are a few of the most popular auction sites besides eBay.

- *Bidville.com.* This site promotes itself as "an alternative to eBay." It does not charge listing fees, but rather a "final success fee" based on a percentage of the sale price. If an item doesn't sell, no charges are assessed unless you opted for some of the "enhancement fees" such as bold or featured highlights. Overall, Bidville.com's fees are less than eBay's, but the site is not quite as user- or search-friendly. And while the site is growing, it still has a mere fraction of the number of registered users as eBay—not great for sellers, but it could mean some excellent bargains for shoppers.

- *Amazon.com.* Amazon offers three different programs for sellers. The first—and most popular—is Amazon's Marketplace, a specialty site for books, videos, software, and DVDs, where items are listed for a fixed amount. Many shoppers will check this site before going to eBay or another retail store. There is no bidding, so set your prices to effectively compete against other sellers–including Amazon itself. Amazon calculates and collects predetermined shipping fees on each sale and credits a portion of that amount to the seller. If the actual shipping costs will exceed the amount Amazon collects, include the difference in the amount you charge for the product.

  One of the best features about the Marketplace is that shoppers looking for a specific product on Amazon's general retail site will also be pointed to the Marketplace pages—a bonus for sellers. Closing fees are a little higher than Half.com (eBay's fixed-price specialty site for books, movies, games, CDs, computers, and electronics). Also, items on Half.com remain listed indefinitely or until sold; Amazon's Marketplace removes listings after 60 days.

  The second is Amazon's auction site, which has hundreds of categories but generates significantly less traffic than eBay or Yahoo!. To attract sellers, Amazon's auction fees are extremely competitive.

  Amazon's third seller program is zShops, which are similar to eBay stores. There is no fee for the zShop; however, to qualify for a zShop, Amazon requires sellers to be Pro Merchant Subscribers (an auction management system designed for Amazon sellers). This means the cost of the "free" zShop can be as much as three times the cost of a basic eBay store, and the market they reach is much smaller.

- *Yahoo.com*. There was a time when Yahoo! was one of eBay's strongest competitors—and then the site started charging fees and the result was a 50 plus percent drop in auction listings. Because of the Yahoo! site's overall popularity, auction traffic has been slowly rebuilding, but still doesn't come close to eBay's stream of daily visitors. Yahoo!'s listing and closing fees are competitive with eBay, and they offer some additional attractive features. One is the Auction Booth, which is essentially an enhanced "About Me" page with a short URL that subscribers can use in promotion materials.

eBay Still Rules

Though other auction sites are struggling to catch up, eBay remains the world's leader in online auctions, evidenced by the fact that more than 700 million pages are viewed and 120 million searches are conducted daily. With more than 2,500 categories and an estimated 25 million items listed for sale on any given day, eBay is a mecca for both sellers looking for customers and buyers looking for bargains. The best, easiest, and most fun way to learn eBay is to start shopping.

CHAPTER 2

Savvy Shopping on eBay

O NCE CONSIDERED THE WEB'S LARGEST garage sale, eBay is no longer just a dumping ground for used clothing and discarded household furnishings. These days, at least 50 percent of listed auctions are for products labeled "new." The products of virtually every top designer show up routinely; in fact, eBay is considered a fashion emporium and has its own fashion consultant. For goods ranging from collectibles to small appliances to business equipment and even bulldozers, an increasing number of armchair shoppers look first on eBay before checking out an online or brick-and-mortar store. This chapter focuses primarily on auction-buying techniques, but there are plenty of great deals and unique items on eBay that are sold through fixed-price listings or in eBay stores, where bidding is not part of the process.

Successful eBay sellers start by shopping and continue to shop on eBay. In the beginning, it's a good way to see how the system works and how other sellers operate. Also, says David Wombacher (eBay User ID: camerahunter), "It's the best way to build up your feedback. A seller with 25-plus feedback to start will do better than someone with none."

To bid or buy on eBay, you must first register. That you have invested in a book on how to make money selling on eBay suggests you have already done that, but just in case you haven't, do it now. Just go to www.ebay.com, look for the box that says "Welcome New Users," click on "Register Now," and follow the simple steps. Most eBay sellers accept payment through PayPal, an online payment service and eBay subsidiary that allows you to pay for items with a credit card or by debiting your bank account. Opening a PayPal account is easy and free; just go to www.pay pal.com, and follow the instructions. With these basic steps out of the way, you're ready to go shopping.

Know Your Seller

A common question asked by people who have never shopped on eBay is, "How do I know I'm dealing with someone who is reputable?" Each eBay listing includes a Seller Information box that will show you the seller's status with eBay and allow you to see what other people have to say about the seller. The box also has links so you can ask the seller a question, view other items the seller has posted, or visit the seller's eBay store if he or she has one. Whenever you are considering bidding on an item or making a fixed-price purchase from a seller you haven't bought from before, take the time to review the information in this box.

Conducting a Successful Search

Whether you are shopping online or in the mall, being a savvy shopper requires knowing how and where to look for the best deal on exactly what you want. This enjoyable knack can be developed and fine-tuned for any shopping enthusiast, and your online selling career will benefit from knowing how to use those skills on eBay.

Using Keywords

Most people use keywords to search on eBay for several reasons, but the biggest is because sellers don't always put items in appropriate categories or in categories where you might think to look. Here's how to do a basic search using keywords:

From the eBay home page (www.ebay.com), type one or more words that best describe the product you are looking for in the search box. For this exercise, let's look for a black Kate Spade handbag. If you type those four words in the search box, your results will bring up the results matching that criterion. This search will pull up new and used handbags, as well as any multicolored ones that have the word "black" in the title. You can narrow the results by going to the top of the search results page and adding the word "new" or "NWT" (new with tag) to the search criteria. You can also streamline this search further by going to the sidebar on the Search Results page and entering additional information, such as price range, desired material, style, or other specifics.

Of course, multicolored or two-toned handbags are still going to pop up in these searches unless you exclude those words. You can do that by including in the search string a minus sign (–) in front of the excluded words like this: –multi, –two, or –plaid. Use this format for any words you want to eliminate from your search.

If you want two or more words searched in a specific order, place quotations around the phrase (for example, "black Kate Spade handbag"). However, if the seller hasn't used that exact phrase in the title, this approach can eliminate many auctions you might want to see. You can also fine-tune keyword searches by using the Refine Search feature on the Search Results page.

Broaden Your Search

By default, eBay conducts keyword searches on auction titles only. You can get more results by checking the Search Title and Description box below the Keyword box. You may be surprised at how often the keyword you're searching with isn't in a title but appears in the description because the seller thought other words were more appropriate or important to include in the limited space of the title. For example, you may be searching for a man's gold and diamond watch. The seller could title the auction "Brand New Men's Designer Watch" and in the body of the description mention that the watch is gold and diamond. If you search using titles only, you'll miss this listing.

Another way to broaden your search is to use a "wildcard" or asterisk (*) after a keyword. For example, if you search for *possum**, your results will include listings with the words: opossum, o'possum, possums or possum's. Once you have that broad list, you can streamline your search by adding other criteria or excluding certain words from that search.

You can also use the wildcard to eliminate specific groups of words from your search. For example, if you're looking for a list of Craftsman products other than tools, put a minus sign in front of the word "tool" and an asterisk after it, like this: *Craftsman -tool**. Your results will exclude Craftsman products with the whole or partial word tool in the name, such as tools, toolbox, toolbag, toolset, toolkit, etc.

Searching within Categories

Unless you specify a category when you conduct a keyword search, your results will list items from all over the eBay world. For instance, if you typed "white oleander" in the search box, the results would include movies, books, soundtracks, and shrubs. But if you are just looking for the film of that title on DVD, select the DVD category before conducting your search. Narrow your search even further by specifying "new" or "factory sealed" DVDs.

Using eBay's myriad of categories and subcategories is just like shopping from a catalog with all the products conveniently tucked in various sections. Categories can be accessed from the home page, by clicking the "Buy" or "Browse" link at the top of any eBay page, or from any auction listing by clicking the category links at the beginning of the description. Once you are in the desired section or category, you can streamline your search by typing specific keywords in the search box.

Search by Seller or Store

All auction descriptions give you the option to "view seller's other items" by clicking on a link in the Seller Information box. When your keyword search brings up something you're looking for, you may find that seller has similar or additional items that you are also interested in. If you buy more than one item from a particular seller and everything can be shipped together, your shipping costs will naturally be less than if each item is shipped separately. Most sellers pass this savings along to their customers; in eBay language, sellers say they will "combine shipping" on multiple purchases. It's a win-win deal: You save money on shipping, and the seller makes an additional sale.

Once you know a seller, you can routinely search on his User ID to see what he's offering, or you can visit his eBay store if he has one. Do this with the Refine or Advanced Search feature. eBay does not provide a search tool once you are on the list of a particular seller's current offerings; however, you can use the Ctrl-F function (search in top window) to find items by keywords.

Misspellings Spell B-A-R-G-A-I-N-S

Bargains on eBay often come as a result of misspellings—and you can use these mistakes to your advantage. Because the majority of auction shoppers search by keyword rather than category, when a seller makes a mistake in the spelling of the item's name, the listing won't be easy to find. And the items not being viewed and bid on by others are likely to sell at a bargain price to one of the few shoppers savvy enough to find them.

The best way to search for misspellings is to think about different mistakes a seller might make when writing the title or description for his items. Then type those misspelled words into the search box and see what kind of results you get.

Let's say you're looking for an inscribed first edition of *Feeding the Lions*, a 1942 cookbook from the Algonquin Hotel. This rare vintage item commonly sells for prices as high as $500. But if the seller carelessly typed *Feding the Lions* in the title, many collectors would overlook the listing, and it's possible the closing bid could be a fraction of the item's true value. Along the same lines, if you search on "recip," your results will not only include reciprocating saws, but also several cookbook listings that have the word "recipes" misspelled.

You can also use a wildcard or asterisk (*) to find misspellings in auction titles. You could search for typos such as "algon*" for Algonquin, or "feed* the liions" for *Feeding the Lions*. There are lots of clever, creative ways to discover these hidden bargains, and it won't take you long to develop a special search list to use on a regular basis specifically for these typos.

Who's Your Shadow?

Shadowing (watching other bidders) is a favorite pastime of a growing number of eBay shoppers. This is another way to find some good bargains that may be flying under the radar. If you are new to bidding on eBay, it can also teach you some new search skills as you watch how others find things that you have a similar interest in.

It's easy to shadow another bidder. On every auction description page, the history shows how many bidders have bid on that item to date. Click on that link to see a list of all the bidders (which is available except when the auction is private; in that case, only the seller knows who the bidders are). To decide who to shadow, choose either the high bidder or a bidder with a relatively high feedback number, which indicates she is an experienced eBayer. Make a note of her User ID, go to an advanced search page (which can be accessed from almost any eBay page), and click the "Find items by bidder" link. Enter a User ID and decide if you want to see all the current auctions the bidder is interested in or just the ones she is the high bidder on. You can also look at closed auctions she has bid on.

This search will pull up a list of auctions, some of which may be of interest to you. As you look at those listings, note which ones escaped your notice during your own search query and figure out why. Was it something in the title or description? Perhaps a misspelled word or extra detail you didn't include in your search criteria?

Keep in mind that the flip side to shadowing bidders is that someone may want to shadow you. To keep others from seeing what items you're interested in, which potentially draws attention to that auction and could raise the bid, don't place a bid until near the close of the auction. Use the "Watch this item" link to make it easy to monitor the auction.

Save Your Searches

Once you have a search defined exactly the way you want it, save it by clicking on the "Add to Favorites" link. That specific search will be filed in your My eBay section. You can either check it on your own schedule, or have eBay send you an e-mail notification when new auctions have been posted that match your parameters.

You can also save your Favorite Categories, Favorite Sellers, and Favorite Stores, and store them in My eBay. By doing this, whenever you want to access one of your favorites, you can either go to My eBay or use the "Shortcuts to My Favorites" drop-down menu found at the bottom of most eBay pages.

Of course, you can simply bookmark a search page and save it on your computer. But when you use this method, eBay cannot help you keep track of your favorites.

Before You Bid

Once you find an item you want, you're ready to bid—right? Wrong. There are a few things you should do before placing a bid.

Know the value of the item that is being auctioned before placing a bid. If it's a new item, find out what you could buy it for in a store or from another online source. If it's used or refurbished, the value will be less than new, but the actual amount will vary depending on the product itself. Along with knowing the true value of an item, think about how much you're willing to pay for it.

Read the entire auction description carefully. Pay attention to the seller's terms and conditions, and make sure they're acceptable. For example, some sellers will only accept certain payment methods; some restrict where they will ship; some require that a new bidder with minimal feedback contact them before bidding.

What kind of guarantee does the seller offer? What is his return policy? Certainly it's understandable that used items are sold "as is," but an "all sales are final" policy could be a red flag about the type of customer service the seller provides. Decide if you're willing to take the risk of not being happy with your purchase. Most sellers will allow you to return an item for a refund of the purchase price (but not shipping charges) if you are dissatisfied.

If you have any questions about the item or the terms, ask before bidding. If a picture was not provided or is fuzzy, e-mail the seller for a clear photo. If the description does not provide enough details, ask for more.

If delivery time is important, find out in advance what the approximate delivery date will be. You can usually determine this by the type of shipping the seller uses and how soon after the close of the auction she will ship. Most sellers state their shipping procedures in the auction description or on their About Me page, but if you can't find that information, ask.

Once you know what you're bidding on, are comfortable with the seller and the seller's terms, and have decided what the item is worth to you, it's time to get in the game.

Let the Bidding Begin

The bidding process on eBay is simple: just click on "Place Bid" and follow the prompts. Your bid is a legal contract—a commitment to purchase the item at the specified price if you are the winner of the auction. Don't bid unless you're serious about buying.

There are a few circumstances in which a bid can be retracted. If you make an error when entering your bid—for example, you meant to bid $10.50 and acciden-tally typed $105.00—you may retract that bid, but you must immediately re-enter the correct amount. If the description of an item changes substantially after you've bid on it, you may retract your bid. You may also retract a bid if you have tried unsuccessfully to reach the seller by phone or e-mail. And, of course, if someone places a bid using your User ID, that bid can be retracted.

Some bidders will decide they don't want an item after winning an auction and simply not pay for it. This is a violation of the contract you agreed to when you placed your bid, and it's also a violation of eBay's policies.

There are two ways to bid on eBay. You can manually place each bid as the auc-tion progresses, or you can use eBay's automatic system known as proxy bidding.

If you were at a traditional auction, you would call out your bids to the auc-tioneer until you reached your maximum amount or until everyone else stopped bidding and you won the auction. That's essentially what you would be doing by manually bidding on eBay.

But let's say you couldn't go to a particular auction and there was something there that you wanted. So you ask a friend—a proxy—to go and bid on your behalf. You'd tell the proxy what your maximum bid is, and the proxy would place incre-mental bids until either winning the auction or until the bids exceeded your limit.

eBay's system works much the same way. When you place your bid, you can enter the maximum amount you're willing to pay. The system places bids on your behalf, bidding only as much as is necessary to maintain your position as the high bidder until it reaches your maximum amount.

Whether you are bidding manually or using the proxy system, eBay will notify you by e-mail if you are outbid. At that point, you can decide if you want to increase your bid or let the item go. This is the time when you are at greatest risk of catching auction fever, which could spark a bidding war that drives the final price up far past the item's true value. When Rhonda Haney (eBay User ID: 7713November) was selling memorabilia related to Canadian actor Roy Dupuis, she had one regular buyer who chronically suffered from auction fever. Said Haney, "It was an obsession with her. She drove the prices up. She paid more than $200 for one magazine and $1,000 for a set of black-and-white photos." Haney purchased the magazine from the publisher for a few dollars and paid the photographer a percentage of the final sale price.

Regardless of how you choose to bid, keep in mind that most people bid in whole, round numbers such as $12 or $25. Entering an odd number, such as $12.39 or $25.07, will increase your chances of outbidding someone by just a few pennies.

Sniping

Besides being the name of a species of birds, the traditional meaning of the word "snipe" is to shoot at individuals from a concealed place. On eBay, it means to place a high bid in the closing seconds of an auction so that other bidders don't have time to bid again. It's sneaky, but valid—and part of what makes auction buying so much fun.

One way to avoid getting sniped is to place a proxy bid for the full amount you're willing to pay. If the sniper bids less than that amount, your bid will be increased automatically. Although this is a safe alternative to manual bidding, it has its drawbacks. Many experienced bidders feel that bidding early calls attention to an item and encourages other buyers to place bids and drive up the price. In fact,

SMALL BUSINESSES ARE BIG eBAY SHOPPERS

eBay is more than a shopping playground for consumers. Small businesses in all industries are turning to the eBay marketplace for the equipment, supplies, and resources they need to start, operate, and grow their companies. Between 2002 and 2003, business buying on eBay doubled—from $1 billion to $2 billion in global gross merchandise sales.

eBay is adding new services to help address issues small businesses often face, including improving cash flow, hiring, and shipping. For more information about the latest eBay small business services, go to www.ebaybusiness.com.

many serious eBayers won't bid until the final few minutes of an auction to keep the final price as low as possible. If you decide to take this approach, use the "watch this item" link to monitor the auction in your My eBay section. You can also browse your favorite categories using the "ending soonest" sort feature.

Serious snipers often use programs that will place their last-minute bids. Some of the most popular are: eSnipe (www.esnipe.com); PowerSnipe (www.power snipe.com), AuctionBlitz (www.auctionblitz.com), and AuctionSniper (www.auction sniper.com). There's a charge for these services, of course, but users swear their savings more than make up for the cost of the sniping service.

Things to Watch Out For

More than 99 percent of the transactions on eBay are conducted with honesty and integrity. But there are some unscrupulous sellers who will try to take advantage of an unwary buyer—don't let yourself be an easy mark for them.

Check Feedback

eBay's feedback system allows every buyer and seller to post a comment about every completed transaction. The comments can be categorized as positive, neutral, or negative, and eBay automatically calculates a feedback score based on a point system. After a seller's User ID, you'll see a number in parentheses; this is the feedback score, which is the number of eBay members who are satisfied doing business with a particular member. In the Seller Information box, you'll see a positive feedback percentage. This is essentially the satisfied customer ratio; it's calculated by dividing the number of members who have left positive feedback by the number of members who have left both positive and negative feedback. Generally, a feedback percentage of 98 or higher is acceptable, although you might consider buying from a seller with a lower percentage if you check him out carefully. Because this is a percentage figure, keep in mind that the feedback percentage of a relatively new seller with just a few transactions can be seriously skewed by one negative post. Also, when considering the feedback rating, pay attention to whether the feedback applies to purchases or sales—if most of the feedback is in response to the user's buying activities, you can't tell much about his integrity as a seller.

When the positive feedback percentage is anything less than 100, check to see when the negative feedback was posted (if it was a long time ago, the seller may have made some mistakes and mended his ways; if it was recent, it could be a red flag), exactly what was said, and if the user posted a response. You should be able to tell if this was a simple misunderstanding, an honest mistake, or an intentional attempt to cheat someone.

A Picture Is Worth . . .

Think carefully before bidding on or buying an item without a picture. A picture is the best way to know that the seller actually has what he is selling, and it's the best way for you to be sure the item is what is being described. If the listing doesn't include a picture, ask the seller to send you one.

Look carefully at each photograph the seller has posted. Does it match the description? Does it appear to be blurry or doctored? Check some of the seller's current and previous auctions to see if the photo is a duplicate of similar auctions he has posted. If so, you are probably not looking at an actual picture of the item up for sale. Some sellers will lift photos from other auctions, web sites, and even print catalogs. Though this is usually a copyright violation, it's often done more due to laziness and ignorance than dishonesty.

If you have any doubts or questions about what you see in the photo, ask the seller for clarification or a picture of the item at a different angle. If the seller is using a digital camera, this shouldn't be a problem. And the manner and time in which they reply will give you more insight into their reliability.

Inflated Shipping Costs

One of the biggest scams on eBay is grossly inflated shipping and handling fees. This is when sellers charge far more than it actually costs them to package and ship an item, essentially building some profit into their shipping charges. We heard of one case where a seller listed a paint gun for sale with a one-cent Buy It Now price plus $75 shipping. That's unusually blatant; you're more likely to see something like a watch listed at $2 with a shipping cost of $15. Actual shipping and handling costs within the United States for something the size of a watch are likely to be in the $3 to $4 range, including packing and insurance.

You may figure that the watch is worth $17, so you're willing to pay the shipping fee. But the practice is unethical and against eBay policies because the seller's final value fees (what eBay charges the seller when the auction closes) are based on the merchandise price alone. Also, it's standard practice to not refund shipping fees when an item is returned, so if you're not happy with this watch that cost you a total of $17, you'll likely only get $2 refunded if you send it back.

Many sellers like to start auctions at ridiculously low prices in the hope of attracting more buyers, which is an acceptable and effective practice. However, when they try to ensure themselves added profit by charging excessive shipping fees, they're demonstrating a lack of integrity that should make you wary of dealing with them.

Always look at shipping costs and keep them in mind as you calculate the maximum amount you are willing to pay for an item.

Bidding and Selling History

If you have questions or suspicions about a listing, check out the seller's bidding history (use the shadowing techniques explained earlier) to see if the seller is trying to unload something he recently bought from another auction on eBay. If so, you can contact the original seller to find out more about the situation, or ask the current seller directly what is going on. It could be something sneaky—or it could be something as simple as a garment not fitting correctly or not knowing that the spouse had purchased a duplicate fly fishing rod as a surprise gift. But the real surprise will be letting the seller know that you know what he's been up to.

When It's Over

At the close of an auction, eBay sends a notice to all bidders letting them know that the auction has closed, what the final sale price was, and whether or not they won. Most sellers will also send an immediate notification to the winner with payment details. To avoid negative feedback or a non-paying bidder complaint, pay promptly. If for any reason you can't pay promptly, communicate with the seller to make appropriate arrangements.

When the item arrives, leave appropriate feedback for the seller. Assuming you are satisfied, offer a specific positive statement, such as "fast shipping," "great communications," or "exactly as described," letting other buyers know what kind of service to expect from that seller. Many sellers will not leave feedback for you until you have left theirs, so don't delay.

You may choose to leave neutral feedback if the product was satisfactory but the seller did not communicate well or ship promptly. Reserve negative feedback for unsatisfactory situations such as gross misrepresentation or the seller not shipping the product.

The seller should also leave feedback for you. Because positive feedback is so important on eBay, don't be shy about asking a seller to post feedback—especially after you have paid for and received the item, and left feedback for the seller.

If the Seller Fails to Perform

Though most eBay transactions go smoothly, there may be a time when you don't receive what you were expecting or the item is defective. If this happens, look at the seller's return policy again (auction description or About Me page) to see what recourse you have. The majority of sellers will let you return an item for a refund within a certain number of days, minus the shipping fees. You may be able to recover the shipping fees if the item was misrepresented in the auction description or damaged during shipping.

Before leaving feedback, send the seller a nonconfrontational note explaining why you are dissatisfied and ask if he will accept a return. Most sellers will try to work with you to bring the transaction to a satisfactory conclusion, and when that happens be sure to reward them with positive feedback.

Unfortunately, there are a handful of sellers who really don't care what your problem is—you have it, you own it, deal with it. To them, "all sales are final" means "you are stuck." If the seller is uncooperative and is truly at fault, you are not totally without recourse. If you used a credit card or PayPal, dispute the charge. If you believe fraud was involved, report the seller to eBay. And, of course, you can always leave negative feedback to alert other bidders to the potential for problems with a particular seller.

Use Your Tools

The eBay Toolbar is a collection of handy tools primarily used by bidders and sits on your desktop as a single block of buttons. The tools include links to My eBay, favorite search pages, PayPal, and other handy links, as well as security features.

The Toolbar keeps a history of the last 25 eBay searches you've done, even if you don't save them. It also lets you opt to receive desktop alerts for items you are bidding on or watching, even when you're not signed on to eBay. From the Toolbar you can immediately see what items you have won and go directly to PayPal to send a payment. The Bookmark feature works exactly like the Favorites menu on Internet Explorer, where you can save your favorite searches. And the Top Links can quickly take you to other relevant pages, such as Google or the U.S. Postal Service.

Check the eBay site for complete and current details on system requirements and features.

Can't Find It?

Use eBay's Want It Now feature to create a post describing what you're looking for. Your post will include a title that focuses on the keywords that will clearly spell out what you want and a description that is as specific as possible so sellers can match their listings to your request without wasting your or their time. Choose a category and launch your post.

Sellers (or even other eBay members) who have what you're looking for can send you a link to their eBay listing so you can see the item and decide if you want to bid or buy. Want It Now posts remain on eBay for 30 days, or may be deleted sooner if you no longer want to receive responses.

The Want It Now link is on eBay's home page under specialty sites. Once you start selling on eBay, you should regularly browse the Want It Now listings under your category to identify prospective customers.

Practice Makes Perfect

Once you've done some shopping on eBay and you're comfortable with how the site works, it's time to start selling. Use the Buyer's Checklist (Figure 2.1) to help you understand what steps to take before placing a bid, and what to do when the auction closes and you are the winning bidder.

FIGURE 2.1: **BUYER'S CHECKLIST**

BEFORE YOU BID

❏ Determine the item's value.

❏ Check the seller's feedback.

❏ Carefully read the auction description. Does it provide sufficient information? If not, contact the seller for additional details.

❏ Study the photograph. Is it clear enough to show you what you're bidding on?

❏ Check the shipping and handling fees.

❏ Determine the maximum amount you are willing to pay, including shipping costs.

❏ Check the seller's shipping schedule.

❏ Check the seller's return policy, guarantees, and other customer satisfaction policies.

❏ Check the payment options, and be willing to pay via a means the seller accepts.

❏ Only bid if you are serious about purchasing the item. Your bid is a legally binding contract.

AFTER THE AUCTION

❏ Pay promptly.

❏ Provide the seller with any special shipping instructions or other information that may be necessary.

FIGURE 2.1: **BUYER'S CHECKLIST**, continued

❏ If there is a problem (for example, if the item does not arrive, arrives damaged, or is otherwise unsatisfactory), contact the seller to try to resolve the situation.

❏ When you have received the item and are satisfied with your purchase, post positive feedback.

❏ Leave neutral or negative feedback only as a last resort if you are unable to resolve issues with the seller.

CHAPTER 3

Getting Set Up as an eBay Seller

WITH EVERYTHING YOU HAVE TO DO to start a business selling on eBay—creating your business entity, deciding what to sell, setting up your physical operation, etc.—getting set up as an eBay seller is probably the simplest part of the process. eBay's growth is driven by having plenty of great items available for people to buy, and the way to do that is to be attractive to sellers. It's a concept eBay has mastered well, and the advantage is yours.

The first step is to create a seller's account. The process is free, but eBay does require that you provide certain information (a credit or debit card and checking account information) that can be verified. This helps keep the eBay community safe for all users. You'll also need to decide how you're going to pay your seller fees; you can have them deducted from your checking account or charged to a credit card.

As an added measure of security for buyers, sellers can take the extra step of becoming "ID Verified." This process cross-checks your personal information against consumer and business databases for veracity. It takes about ten minutes, and you'll be charged $5 when the process is complete. It is *not* a credit check; eBay is just confirming your identity. When your ID has been verified, an icon will be

CAN YOU REGISTER AS A SELLER WITHOUT A CREDIT CARD?

Though the standard eBay seller registration process requires that you provide a valid credit card number and bank account information that eBay uses to collect seller fees, some users either can't or won't do that. There are those people who don't have credit cards, either by choice or due to financial troubles. Others are simply reluctant to have automatic withdrawals made from their bank accounts or charges made to their credit cards.

If you do not want to place your bank account and credit card information on file with eBay but you still want to register as a seller, you can use the ID verification process for a cost of $5 and set up an alternative arrangement for paying seller fees.

ID Verify simply confirms that you are who you say you are. It is not a credit check, and eBay doesn't care if you've been late making car payments or have other blemishes on your credit record. However, because eBay will be unable to automatically collect your seller fees, a $25 limit will be placed on your selling account. When the fees due exceed $25, you will not be allowed to post items for sale until your account is paid.

You can make payments by check, money order, PayPal, or a one-time credit card payment. If you're serious about your eBay business, you might want to prepay your account to avoid service interruptions.

If you change any of the information originally provided when establishing your proof of identity, such as name, address, or phone number, you will need to reapply and go through the ID verification process again.

placed next to your User ID. New eBay users with minimal feedback may find that being ID verified gives other users more confidence about dealing with them.

What's in a Name?

Your User ID is the name by which you'll be known on eBay. Choosing it is equivalent to choosing a business or brand name for yourself. Your User ID should describe you, your interests, or your niche in a way that will be instantly recognizable and easy to remember. Some members choose unusual, but memorable IDs that reveal a quirky sense of humor such as roadkillwoman or not-the-daddy. Fine for a shopper or even an occasional seller, but when you are running a business, your name should reflect what you do. Bob Bidwell (eBay User ID: plates-n-stuff) chose an ID that reflects his area of expertise in limited-edition plates and other collectibles. And it's not hard to guess that Maggie Donapel (eBay User ID: plums books) specializes in books.

eBay allows users to have more than one ID; in fact, you can have as many User IDs as you have valid e-mail addresses, as long as none of them have been suspended for any reason. If you have more than one specialty area, you may want a User ID for each one. Or you may have one ID for buying and another for selling.

Ron and Sheri Walker (eBay User IDs: beansantiques and painlesstransactions) have two User IDs for selling purposes. They use beansantiques (from the name of their brick-and-mortar antique store) for selling antiques and collectibles. Incidentally, their eBay business was so successful that they closed that store not long after they began selling on eBay. The Walkers created a second User ID, painlesstransactions, under which they sell items that are not considered antiques or collectibles—primarily clothing and accessories. They chose the name because they wanted people to feel comfortable buying from them. Ron says, "Painlesstransactions is an inviting name. It says in your mind, 'this is easy, and it won't hurt me.'"

Gary Neubert (eBay User ID: gatorpack) uses different User IDs for selling and buying. His reasoning is that he wants to protect his seller ID feedback rating, which is 100 percent positive. But if he is involved in a negative transaction as a buyer and there is a dispute, he doesn't want his perfect selling record marred by a sour deal. He says, "I would hate to get a negative feedback in retaliation for a feedback [I left for a seller] that was justly deserved for a buying activity that doesn't have anything to do with our business."

Power Seller Karen Kelley (eBay User ID: thepinkboutique) chose a User ID that reflected her personality, her favorite color, and the nature of her business, which is women's clothing. She says, "I am very theme-oriented, and that is why everything has kind of revolved around my User ID. The connotation that visitors get when they think of The Pink Boutique is pretty, feminine, and girly, in a welcoming little clothing boutique."

Your User ID must be between two and 20 characters, and may contain letters, numbers, and/or some symbols. It cannot contain spaces or tabs, nor can it be obscene, profane, or in violation of any of eBay's guidelines. Also, it cannot be an e-mail address or a web site, although some folks try to get around this by including symbols in their ID such as: **www.mysite.com**. This may seem like a bright idea; however, it's against eBay policy and you're likely to get caught. It's better to find a short, clever nickname that identifies you and is not in danger of being suspended.

Start by brainstorming a list of IDs that could work for you. With millions of registered users on eBay, it's possible your first choice—or even your first few choices—will have been taken. Look for variations on your initial idea, even something as simple as rearranging the words or making a few minor changes. For example, let's say your name is Sam and you sell handmade wood furniture. Your list of potential IDs could include samsfurniture, furniturebysam, handmadefurniture, samswoodfurniture, designsbysam, and so on. If you want to see if a particular User ID is available before you register, do a search by seller.

Because IDs can't include spaces, insert a hyphen or an underscore to separate words, such as big_tom or the-fuzzy-dog. Use numbers with discretion and only when they make sense. For instance, recipes4me or 123stop are easy to remember; barry846921 is not. Also, remember that every ID is displayed in lower case. Type out your ideas and look at them to be sure they are clear and don't inadvertently give the wrong impression. For example, Brad and Carol sell antiques so they choose the ID of bandcantiques. They know they were thinking "B and C Antiques," but you would probably read it as "band can tiques." Or how about an arts-and-crafts supply seller who wants to operate under the name US Expressions? You might see that when you look at usexpressions; but you might also see "u sex pressions" or "use x pressions."

If running the words together might be confusing to someone who doesn't know what you do, separate the words for clarity. Brad and Carol's ID would be far more clear if they added hyphens like this: b-and-c-antiques. Check out eBay's Help section for more tips on selecting a User ID.

Although you are allowed to change your ID once every 30 days, avoid doing so unless it's absolutely essential. Regular customers who get to know you by one ID may not be able to find you if you change. Atlanta-based scrapbook and craft supplies seller Kathy Logan (eBay User ID: rosie_peachstate) says she has seen some sellers change their User ID every couple of months, and it raises issues of distrust. "People often change their User ID because something went wrong with the other one," she says. If, for example, someone accumulates a substantial amount of negative feedback, he may decide to just start over with a new identity—"like a witness-protection program," says Logan. Although this is certainly not always the case, it's important to find a good User ID in the beginning and stick with it.

Decide How to Get Paid

What payment methods will you accept? Decide this in advance, because it's something many bidders consider before placing a bid. Your payment terms should be clearly stated in your auction listings and in your eBay store if you have one. Without question, electronic payments (credit cards, debit cards, and e-checks) are the most popular methods of paying for auction goods because they are faster, safer, and easier to process and track than other methods. But don't make your decision based solely on what's best and easiest for *you*; consider what will make you an attractive seller to potential bidders and buyers, and come up with a payment method package that will contribute to your success.

PayPal

eBay's subsidiary PayPal (www.paypal.com) is the site's preferred payment method and the most popular online payment service. PayPal is free to buyers and allows them to pay with their credit card, debit card, bank account, or PayPal balance without revealing their private financial information to the seller.

PayPal has three levels of accounts. If you're serious about selling on eBay, set up a PayPal Business Account that allows you to send and receive money in the name of your company. You will pay a transaction fee to receive payments, but the overall cost is less than setting up credit card merchant accounts.

New eBay sellers often resist paying that expense. PayPal's personal account allows you to receive funds through bank account payments with no charge, but does not allow you to accept credit card payments, and some sellers feel this is adequate. But it eliminates all the people who only want to pay with a credit card— and that's a huge portion of your potential market. Other new eBay sellers simply don't accept PayPal at all—a guaranteed way to lose sales.

Some sellers try to recover the PayPal fees by charging a handling fee in that amount, but this violates eBay's policy prohibiting imposing a surcharge for payments made through any electronic money service.

The best approach is to view the PayPal fee as a cost of doing business—and remember, you don't pay it unless you sell something.

BidPay

BidPay (www.bidpay.com) is an online payment system that is free for sellers but buyers must pay to make payments. Sellers receive funds two ways: either deposited into a checking account or via a Western Union money order issued by BidPay and mailed to the seller. Because buyers must pay a fee, BidPay is not as popular as PayPal. However, this is a great alternative for, and is used more often by, international buyers who want to pay by money order.

Personal Checks

Some sellers are reluctant to accept personal checks because of the risk that the check might bounce. The real reason to avoid personal checks is that they're a nuisance to handle. Most sellers say bad checks are rarely a problem, and many don't even bother to wait for the check to clear before shipping an item. Georgene Harkness (eBay User ID: mynewthreads) says she has only held an auction item once because of a personal check. "The lady told me in advance that her check was going to bounce because of problems with her checking account," Harkness said. "So I held her item until the funds were available and the check cleared, but that has been the only time there was a problem."

If a buyer wants to pay by check, you have to wait for the check to be mailed to you, then deposit it into your account (which means paperwork and a trip to the bank), then wait for it to clear (if that's your policy) before shipping the merchandise. Certainly you want to think carefully before deciding to refuse personal checks—although this is a policy some sellers have established. You can always direct buyers who want to pay by check to PayPal, to have an electronic check issued. It usually takes only three to four days for the funds to be deposited into your account.

Money Orders and Cashier's Checks

There is little risk in accepting money orders, cashier's checks, and other forms of certified funds. In the unlikely event that the check is lost in the mail, the buyer can initiate a trace and replacement. The biggest drawback to this payment method is the same as with personal checks: it adds time to the transaction and involves more paperwork for you.

The primary risk you have in accepting this type of payment is the possibility that the money order or cashier's check could be forged, stolen, or fraudulent in some other way. Be suspicious if any buyer sends you a cashier's check for more than the amount of the purchase and asks you to refund the difference (a common scam). For high-dollar purchases, ask your bank to confirm the validity of the cashier's check with the issuing bank before you ship the merchandise.

Escrow Service

An escrow service is a third party that will collect the payment from the buyer and hold the funds until the merchandise has been delivered and the buyer is satisfied. Escrow services are typically used for high-priced items. The process protects both the seller, who doesn't ship until the funds have been received by the escrow service, and the buyer, because the escrow service holds the funds until he authorizes the payment to be made.

Be sure the escrow company you choose is legitimate and licensed. Escrow scams are fairly easy to pull off, and victims have little recourse. eBay and eBay Motors partner with Escrow.com (www.escrow.com), which accepts payments by credit card, PayPal, check, wire transfer, money order, and cashier's check. The amount of the fee varies depending on the transaction.

Credit Card Merchant Accounts

Some eBay sellers, particularly those who are high-volume and/or have a brick-and-mortar store or other sales venue, choose to accept credit and debit cards by opening merchant accounts. This is a convenience for buyers who prefer to pay by credit or debit card and who do not have or want a PayPal account. Merchant accounts are not as expensive as they used to be, but its likely you'll still pay more per transaction than you will with PayPal. Also, some merchant service providers will limit the total amount of payments you can accept each month, which can be a serious disadvantage to a high-volume seller.

Create an "About Me" Page

eBay encourages sellers to create an About Me page, which is essentially a free online brochure that lets you describe your business, tell buyers what you have to offer, outline your policies, and provide other information that will help your business. eBay provides a number of design templates to help you quickly and easily design a sharp, professional-looking About Me page. Before you set yours up, browse around and read others' About Me pages. Consider the content for your page from the perspective of a potential customer—it should be appealing, easy to understand, and presented in a way that will make someone want to do business with you.

David Wombacher (eBay User ID: camerahunter) uses a simple format for his About Me page that explains his business practices and policies and tells a little about who he is personally. He writes: "Safe delivery of your item is my responsibility, and if something happens I will take care of it. I want this to be a pleasant experience for you and me both." He talks about his wife, four children, faith, hobbies and interests, and professional background. After you read his About Me page, you're as comfortable with him as you are with a merchant down the street from you with whom you chat regularly.

"An About Me page is very important, and it needs to reflect who you really are—not just interests but something about you personally," Wombacher says.

"People really do read them, and what you say there can make a connection with people that will not be easily broken."

Your About Me page may contain a link to, or the web address of, your individual web site, but it may not specifically promote off-eBay sales or sales of items that are prohibited on eBay. For more about setting up an About Me page, see Chapter 11.

Know Your Options

Before you begin posting items for sale, know what your options are for selling on eBay. Spend at least a full day browsing in the site, studying the various auctions, fixed-price listings, and stores. Read the help files and message boards. You'll enjoy greater success faster if you take the time to learn all your options and choose the best strategies for your particular operation.

eBay Stores: The Virtual Alternative to Brick and Mortar

For a small, part-time eBay seller, an eBay store could be helpful, but it's not necessary. But for someone who wants to build a substantial, profitable business selling on eBay, a store is an excellent tool.

An eBay store is a place on eBay where you can display all your listings in one customizable place, encourage multiple purchases from buyers, cross-promote your merchandise, and maintain a larger permanent inventory than you sell through auctions. eBay supports store operators with a variety of promotions, including the store icon in the Seller Information box of every listing that links to your store. The eBay stores directory is designed to promote all stores, and you'll also have your own web address (URL) that you can use as you wish. The Stores E-mail Marketing Tool lets you send e-mails directly to your buyers; you can use this tool to announce new items or specials, or to deliver other information that will propel the buyers on your list into your store to shop.

The process of opening an eBay store is almost as simple as setting up your initial User ID. The only requirements are that you be a registered eBay seller and have a feedback of 20 or higher, or be ID verified, or have a PayPal account in good standing.

Store Levels and Prices

The cost of an eBay store ranges from nominal to substantial, depending on the level you choose. Check the web site for current rates. The three levels are:

1. *Basic.* Ideal for sellers who are just starting out and want an affordable, easy-to-use platform for online sales, a basic store is automatically listed in the eBay stores directory and will appear in every category directory where you have items listed.

2. *Featured.* Designed for small-to-medium-sized sellers who want to grow their online business, a featured store rotates through a special featured section on the eBay stores home page; receives priority placement in "related stores" on search and listings pages; and is featured within the category directory pages where you have items listed.

3. *Anchor.* The advanced solution for high-volume sellers who want maximum eBay exposure, anchor stores offer the same benefits as featured stores, plus your store can be showcased with your logo within the eBay stores directory pages and will receive premium placement in "related stores" on search and listings pages.

In general, the more you invest in your eBay store—both in level and effort—the more your store sales will be.

Setting Up Your eBay Store

From the eBay home page, click on eBay Stores, then on "Open a Store" and follow the steps to get your store set up. You should come up with a name for your store before you begin this process.

Your eBay store name, which will also be its URL, can be a maximum of 35 characters that will be displayed in lowercase letters. Choose a straightforward name that tells buyers what you sell.

Your store name must start and end with a letter or number; cannot start with four or more consecutive letter A's; cannot start with an E followed by a number; and cannot infringe on any other company's trademark. Your store name can be the same as your User ID, assuming it meets the store name requirements. eBay's Help Center offers additional advice for naming your store.

Keep It Staffed

Your eBay store will be open for business 24/7/365—whether you're awake or asleep, at your computer, or playing golf. Though it doesn't need to be physically staffed around the clock, you need to pay attention to it every day. Monitor your store closely, answer questions from shoppers promptly, ship merchandise on schedule and as promised, and deal with any other customer service issues that might arise as soon as possible.

If you go on vacation or are going to be away for any reason, try to arrange for someone else to monitor the site and take care of your business. If that isn't practical, take advantage of eBay's vacation hold service. You can choose a setting that will hide your store inventory or one that tells shoppers that you are gone and when you will return.

Think about Your Future: Become a Power Seller

Power Sellers are eBay's most successful sellers in terms of product sales and customer satisfaction. To achieve this esteemed designation, a seller has to meet a monthly sales quota and maintain a positive feedback rating of 98 percent or higher. There are five Power Seller levels, each based on gross monthly sales. They are:

1. Bronze
2. Silver
3. Gold
4. Platinum
5. Titanium

Though there is no charge to become a Power Seller, it is not an automatic process. eBay monitors sales activity and each month sends out invitations to qualified sellers. Sellers who accept the invitation appreciate the status that comes with the title. It tells buyers that the seller is serious about her business and committed to upholding eBay's high standards. Kelley says there is prestige and honor behind that little icon. "People look at it and know I can be trusted," she says.

Other perks include enhanced technical and customer support, as well as publications, promotional offers, eBay promotional merchandise, advanced selling education, opportunities to participate in research, and more. Kelley says, "I'm on a silver level, which means I can call eBay 24 hours a day. I've had to do that a couple of times, and it was wonderful being able to talk to someone right when I needed them."

Accepting the Power Seller designation means committing to maintaining a specific monthly sales level and agreeing to the Power Seller Rules, such as having a no-questions-asked return policy. Some high-volume eBay sellers elect to decline the invitation because they don't want to comply with eBay's stringent requirements; some even see those requirements as interference in their business, and reject the Power Seller opportunity for that reason.

Whether you choose to accept the Power Seller invitation is a decision you have to make based on your particular business and operating style. But qualifying for the designation is a worthwhile goal for your eBay operation.

CHAPTER 4

Starting and Managing Your Operation

O NCE YOU DECIDE TO START A BUSINESS using eBay as your sales platform or add eBay selling to an existing operation, you need to take the same standard planning and implementation steps that you would for any other kind of business. That means figuring out exactly what you want to do, creating a plan for it, implementing the plan, and making adjustments as necessary.

If you're tempted to skip this chapter, please don't. This material isn't especially sexy, but it's essential to your eBay business.

Define Your Business

If you already have a business and want to use eBay as a vehicle to increase your sales, this step is easy. If you don't have an existing business, you've got some work to do.

Exactly what kind of business do you want to start and run? "A business on eBay" is not a sufficient answer. There are hundreds of thousands of businesses operating on eBay; each is unique—and for each, the fact that it operates on eBay is only a small part of its description.

Another insufficient answer is, "A business selling popular products with a huge markup." It's certainly nice when a retailer hits a proverbial home run with a product choice, but your chances of success will be far greater if you are working in an area you enjoy.

Do you have something new or better to offer? Do you have something that would appeal to a market segment whose needs are not being adequately met by what is available? Are you going to buy products from other sources, or are you going to handle the manufacturing yourself? Do you know who would buy your products and why they would buy from you over another source? What value can you add to your product that sets you apart from your competitors?

Just because some companies are making millions through eBay sales doesn't mean that your success on eBay will be automatic. So for now, set aside the idea that you're going to be selling on eBay and focus instead on what kind of business you want to have, what products and services you want to offer, who your market will be, and what you can do to give yourself a competitive edge.

Think about how much you have in the way of cash and resources to spend on your business, and recognize that your success will likely be directly proportionate to your investment. Nona Van Deusen (eBay User ID: stylebug.com) started her eBay business as a homebased part-timer. She recalls, "I didn't have anyone to answer to. How much I put into it was what I got out of it." Things are different for her now. She has a commercial location and six employees plus a number of independent contractors. Though she still loves what she does, she's far more serious about it. It's also important to be realistic about how much time it will take for your business to turn a profit.

Michael Jansma (eBay User ID: gemaffair) says he often talks to people who are trying to sell on the internet and complain that they're not making money. They'll talk about spending $10,000 on web site development, $1,000 a month on Google advertising, and thousands more stocking their eBay store, but six months later, they're not showing a profit. Jansma says, "I say to them, 'What if you had taken all that same capital, and you'd gone out and bought a store, hired employees, put in a computer system, brought in products—would you expect to be making money in six months?' They say, 'Well, no.' I say, 'Why is the internet any different?' The idea that you can just put products on the internet and sell them and make money, without any capital investment, without any time investment, is ludicrous. It's a business, just like any other business. I still find it shocking that people think it's this gold mine waiting to be tapped by anybody with any product at any price with any investment. It's not. If you're not as smart and savvy as the rest of the world, you're not going to do well."

Write a Business Plan

With your basic concept defined, you can move on to writing your business plan. eBay offers so many different opportunities that a business plan is essential for you to get and stay focused. A clear business plan lets you take all the wonderful ideas you'll get from this book and other places and organize them into a functioning and profitable operation.

Ideally, you would have a thorough plan on paper before you start your business. So if you're still in the thinking stages, great. Even if you're already buying and selling on eBay, take the time right now to create a plan.

Don't look at this exercise as a chore; it should be an exciting process. When you write down your plans, you have the opportunity to clarify them, think them through, and examine them for consistency and true potential. You'll be able to figure out what you need for start-up and long-term operations. Essentially, your business plan is your action plan, and you need to do the same things to start a business selling on eBay that you would if you were selling in any other venue.

Gary Hunt (eBay User ID: speedwind) says he was too conservative when he started his business. "If I could have done anything different, I would have had a bigger vision to begin with. To get where I am, I took several steps which weren't big enough. For example, as my business grew and I wanted to get out of my house, I bought an office condominium. But I never moved in, because it got too small before I could. And now I have 2,500 square feet, and I already have to move. I didn't think big enough." A detailed business plan may have helped Hunt grow in a pattern more consistent with his sales volume and goals.

Avoid the mistake of writing your plan and then putting it on a shelf to collect dust. This should be a living, breathing document that serves as a road map for your business. Use it as an ongoing guide; refer to it regularly throughout the start-up and during the continuing operation of your company.

Another important reason to have a solid business plan is if you're going to be seeking outside financing, either in the form of loans or investors. This document is the primary tool that will convince funding sources of your venture's worth.

TEST, TEST, TEST

An old Ashanti proverb says, "No one tests the depth of a river with both feet." The point is, don't leap into your eBay business without making sure that what you're going to do will work—and that means testing.

Testing is essential for the success of any business idea. Most products are viable, but you need to determine under what circumstances they will be profitable. The cost of testing is part of your start-up investment. Even though you may be selling products in your testing stage, don't worry about making money on them. The knowledge you'll gain is far more valuable than a 10 or 20 percent profit.

Randy Smythe (eBay User ID: glacierbaydvd) spent a year testing his concept of selling DVDs on eBay to see what auction formats worked best. He says he wasn't concerned about profit; he wanted to figure out what would work.

Test different auction formats, listing designs, description language, photographs, store inventory—whatever you can change, test and track the results. Test your marketing efforts using the same approach. And even after you've completed the testing phase and are up and running, never introduce a new product without testing first.

Whether you want to start a part-time solo eBay business that never gets any larger or build a multimillion-dollar operation, take your time developing your plan. You're making a serious commitment, and there's no need to rush.

Once your plan is complete and you're up and running, give it a thorough review at least once a year. Check to see if you're still on track—if you're not, are you ahead or behind? Figure out what's going on and why, and what you need to do about it. Do you need to change what you're doing, or change the plan?

Laurence J. Peter (author of *The Peter Principle*) said, "If you don't know where you are going, you will probably end up somewhere else." If your destination is a successful eBay business, you need to start with a plan.

Choose a Legal Structure

The choice of legal structure for your business is an important decision that can affect your financial liability, the amount of taxes you pay, and the degree of ultimate control you have over the company, as well as your ability to raise money, attract investors, and ultimately sell the business.

Don't confuse legal structure with operating structure. The legal structure defines ownership of the company. The operating structure determines who makes management decisions and runs things on a day-to-day basis. Your operating structure is far more fluid and easy to change than your legal structure, and it probably will change significantly as you get started and grow your company.

You have four basic choices when it comes to legal structure:

1. Sole proprietorship
2. Partnership
3. Corporation
4. Limited liability company

Sole Proprietorship

This is the simplest and easiest form of business ownership and is used by the majority of companies in the United States. In a sole proprietorship, the business and the owner are one and the same. The owner enjoys all the benefits and accepts all the liabilities of the company—in other words, she is totally responsible for everything related to the company. To become a sole proprietor, you simply have to decide that you are one. But if you want a business that will last beyond your active participation in it, this is not the best form of ownership. In a sole proprietorship, the life of the business is tied to the life of the owner; when the owner either stops operating the business or dies, the business essentially dies.

Partnership

If you are starting your business with one or more other people, you may choose to form an association called a partnership. There are two types of business partnerships: general, in which each partner is an agent of the partnership, each can bind the partnership without the consent of other partners, and each is liable for all the partnership debts; and limited, which allows a certain class of partners to limit their liability to the amount of their investment as long as they do not participate in the management of the organization. If you create a general partnership, you and your partners will likely be active in running the company. If you create a limited liability partnership, it will likely be because someone wants to fund your idea but does not want to participate in the operation.

The most critical element of any partnership is the partnership agreement. This is the document that defines the legal aspects of the partnership and spells out the obligations and responsibilities of each partner. No matter how compatible you think you and your business partners will be, it's a good idea to put everything in writing. The process will confirm your mutual understanding of your goals and methods, and will identify and give you the chance to work out any misunderstandings before they become problems. This is important whether your plans are to start a part-time business buying used items at garage sales and posting them on eBay or you want to grow a substantial enterprise in which eBay is only part of an overall sales strategy.

Corporation

A corporation is a separate legal entity that can own property, can incur debt, and is recognized by the Internal Revenue Service. It is owned by shareholders whose liability is essentially limited to the amount of their investment.

When you form a corporation, you'll need to decide if it's going to be a C or a subchapter S corporation. The difference is a taxation issue, not a structural one. In a C corporation, company profits are taxed at the corporate level and then again at the personal level if they are distributed to shareholders as dividends. The tax process of a subchapter S corporation is more like a partnership or sole proprietorship; you must meet certain IRS requirements regarding the class of stock issued and the number of shareholders to make this election.

Perhaps the most important benefit of forming a corporation is in the area of asset protection. That's the process of making sure that the assets you don't want to put into the business (like your home, car, and personal belongings) don't stand liable for the business debt. To take advantage of the protection a corporation offers, you must respect and maintain the corporation's identity and not mingle it with your own. That means keeping your corporate and personal funds separate, even if you are the sole shareholder, and following your state's rules regarding holding annual meetings and other record-keeping requirements.

Limited Liability Company (LLC)

This business structure option offers many of the protections of a corporation combined with the often more favorable tax status of a partnership. Some states allow a single-owner LLC, but most require two or more owners. LLC owners are called members, and their ownership status is represented by an interest certificate rather than a stock certificate. Another issue to consider is that LLCs have a limited life of about 30 years, in contrast to a sole proprietorship, which ends at the death of the owner, or a corporation that remains "alive" until it is dissolved.

Consider who is going to be involved in your company, how you're going to relate to one another, what you need to do to protect your assets and limit your personal liability if necessary, and how your business structure fits with your tax strategy. Then make your decision. You don't need an attorney to set up your legal structure; there are plenty of excellent do-it-yourself books and kits on the market, and most of the state agencies that oversee corporations and LLCs will provide you with guidelines. Even so, it might be a good idea to consult with an attorney to make sure you haven't overlooked anything and that your documents are complete and will allow you to truly function as you want.

Select a Location

If eBay is going to be your primary sales channel, the process of selecting a location will be simple: you just need a place that has room enough for your inventory and can handle your shipping. But if eBay is just part of your big picture, you'll have other issues to consider. Depending on your specific type of business, you can choose to work from home, open a retail store, or operate from a commercial/industrial facility.

Staying Home

eBay has made it possible for thousands of people to start profitable homebased businesses. Whether you can become one of them will depend on a number of things, including local zoning codes, your landlord (if you rent), your family situation, your budget, and your plans for your company.

Depending on your product, a homebased eBay business can successfully function in a relatively small space, or it can take up a lot of room. You need to set up your desk and computer, plus you'll need an area for staging product photographs, packing and shipping tasks, and storage for your inventory and supplies.

It's ideal if you can set aside a room (or rooms) exclusively for business use. If you can't, do the best you can with the resources you have. Remember that to take the home office deduction on your taxes, the IRS requires that you have a room used solely for business. If you're only using part of a room or your office doubles as a den or guest room, a home office deduction probably wouldn't survive an IRS audit. You can, of course, deduct all other allowable business expenses.

An alternative to being completely homebased is to work from home but rent warehouse space for inventory storage and perhaps your shipping operation. Or you may start from home and then move as your business grows and you need more space.

Retail

You have a number of options if you decide to open a retail store, and your decision will be based on the type of business you have and what you're selling. Understand that the face-to-face retail side of your operation will be very different from the side that operates on eBay.

Commercial/Industrial

If being homebased isn't part of your plan, and you also don't want to have a retail store where customers come in to shop, consider a warehouse or light industrial facility.

If your inventory includes temperature-sensitive items, the facility should be adequately air-conditioned. Other important issues to consider are security and accessibility, especially if you plan to work at night and on weekends.

Wherever you choose to locate, find out what sort of licenses and permits you need before you sign a lease or, if you're going to be homebased, before you start selling. Also, remember that commercial leases are far more complicated than residential leases; make sure you completely understand what you're signing.

Give this Child a Name

One of the most important marketing tools a business has is its name. It should very clearly identify what you do in a way that will appeal to your target market. It should be short, catchy, memorable—and easy to pronounce and spell. When you sell on eBay, you not only need a company name, you also need an eBay User ID (explained in Chapter 3). Make them as close to the same as possible.

Once you've chosen a name, protect it by registering it with the appropriate state agency. Because eBay allows you to do business nationally and even internationally, it's a good idea to register your company name with the U.S. Patent and Trademark Office (PTO). You might even consider trademarking your eBay User ID.

Insure Your Investment

Because it takes so much to start a business, even a small one, protect it with sufficient insurance. Your homeowner's policy likely covers only a minimal amount of business equipment and no inventory or liability; you'll need additional coverage for that. Commercial landlords generally require proof of certain levels of liability insurance and sometimes other types of coverage.

If you accept items on consignment (either as a Trading Assistant, a Trading Post, or just as part of your eBay operation), be sure your insurance covers those items if they are damaged by a covered peril (typically, fire or flood) or stolen while in your possession.

If you manufacture a product that you sell on eBay, whether you're a large industrial operation or a homebased crafter, you need to consider product liability coverage. Should the item you make cause injury or damage, you could be forced to pay.

A big advantage of business liability coverage is that the policy will typically require your insurer to defend you if you are sued—whether or not you are found to be at fault. Read your policy carefully and be sure it includes legal expenses.

Sit down with a commercial insurance agent who is familiar with your type of business; analyze your potential risks and exposures; and then purchase appropriate and adequate coverage.

Operating Hours

One of the big appeals of selling on eBay is that it doesn't really matter when you work as long as you answer e-mails promptly and get your products shipped as promised. Some solo business owners need the discipline of designated operating hours; others like the flexibility of just working until the job is done. Make your choice depending on what suits you best.

If you have partners or employees, you'll need to establish working hours for them. And if you have customers who come to or call your facility, it's a good idea to have regular business hours so they know when to expect your business to be staffed by a live person.

Policies and Procedures

Even the smallest of businesses needs policies and procedures by which to operate. At a minimum, you need to establish procedures for listing your auctions and eBay store items; shipping policies (it could be your policy to always ship within two business days of receiving payment, but never sooner than 24 hours so you have time to be sure the payment is not fraudulent); payment policies (what type of payment you will accept and how long you will wait for a bidder to pay); and merchandise return policies. Put all your policies in writing. If you have a client who is excessively demanding, politely refer to your written policies and stand your ground.

If you have employees, they need to know what the rules are, and you can let them know with clearly defined policies and procedures.

Managing Your Business

Selling on eBay can be a lot of fun, but never lose sight of the fact that this is a business for you—treat it like one. Know what you have to do to make your customers happy and keep them coming back, and do it. Monitor your financial situation and make sure you are meeting or exceeding your revenue and profitability goals. Stay legal—have all the necessary and appropriate licenses and permits, and operate within eBay's guidelines.

Know Your Competition

Take the time to study the other sellers in your category as well as the overall top sellers on eBay. Don't reinvent the wheel—copy the techniques other successful sellers are using (but remember, you can't copy their listings or their photographs without permission). To find eBay's top sellers, visit www.nortica.com, click on "user area," then check out the top eBay sellers based on feedback rating and transaction amount.

Play by the Rules

Perhaps your most important policy is to always follow the eBay policies. It's not hard; in fact, most of it is just common sense. But the consequences for rule violations can range from just having your auction removed to criminal charges. Complete details on eBay polices are on the web site, but here are some key points to keep in mind as you're getting started:

- *Adults only.* eBay requires that all users be at least 18 years old. If your children want to buy and sell things on eBay, you have to do it for them and be responsible for the transaction.
- *Pay promptly.* When you shop on eBay, honor your commitment by paying promptly. Non-paying bidders (bidders who win auctions but fail to pay) will receive two warnings before they are suspended. There may be legitimate reasons for a bidder to fail to complete a transaction, such as serious illness, emergencies, acts of nature, and computer problems. Should something like this happen, do your best to communicate with the seller as quickly as possible. If you are a seller dealing with a non-paying

bidder, report the situation to eBay and request a credit for the final value fee.

- *Be honest and ship promptly.* Significantly misrepresenting an item in your description, not meeting the terms outlined in your listing, or failing to deliver an item for which you accepted payment is not only a violation of eBay policies, it may also be considered criminal fraud.

- *Don't cheat the site.* You may not circumvent eBay fees by using contact information obtained from eBay or any eBay service to complete a sale outside eBay.

- *No threats or profanity.* eBay policies prohibit making threats of physical harm to another user. You may also not use language that is racist, hateful, sexual, or obscene in nature in a public area on eBay.

- *Don't sell or buy prohibited or restricted items.* As an eBay user, you are ultimately responsible for making sure that the items you sell and purchase on eBay are legal according to all applicable jurisdictions and permitted by eBay policies. When the auction involves illegal products or activities, eBay reports the seller to the proper authorities and cooperates with investigations.

- *No shill bidding.* Shilling is an old auction term that means using phony bids to inflate prices—it's against eBay policies, and it's illegal. In one case, a New York eBay seller pled guilty to violating the state's antitrust law and was ordered to pay $50,000 in restitution and fines for shilling on eBay.

Generally, first-time eBay policy violators receive an informational alert explaining the violation and detailing whatever action they need to take that eBay determines to be appropriate and necessary. You may, for example, be asked to change the wording in your listing—or eBay may end the auction and refund your listing fees. In most cases, eBay gives the user the benefit of the doubt. Serious or repeat violations may result in a suspension and possibly a referral to authorities for criminal prosecution.

CHAPTER 5

What Can You Sell and Where Can You Find It?

MANY EBAY SELLERS START OUT BY selling odds and ends they have around the house—a process that often leads spouses to threaten to nail down items they don't want sold. But this is a great learning exercise *and* a great way to get rid of stuff that you'll never miss and you don't want to store or dust anymore. If those items are in good condition, you'll probably get more for them on eBay than by having a garage sale. And because these are items you already own, selling them on eBay is a virtually risk-free way to gain practical eBay experience.

The items you put up on eBay do not have to be in perfect condition. Steve Mack (eBay User ID: ztradingpost) says, "There is a market for broken stuff, too." Fred Johnson (eBay User ID: quikdropflcas) knows that well. His QuikDrop store (a retail store where people can drop off items to be sold on eBay) auctioned a car part (a Dodge Viper supercharger) that had been damaged in shipping. The description clearly described the damage, and it was also evident in the photos. The auction started at 99 cents—and, after 38 bids, closed with a winning bid of $3,600.

If you already have a business, you can, of course, sell on eBay whatever you sell in your store. If you're starting from scratch, choose products you know, have experience with, and are interested in. Make sure they are readily available and that you can handle the storage, packing, and shipping. Be absolutely certain that people are buying.

Just about anything you sell on eBay has the potential to be profitable—or not profitable—depending on how you run your business. Browse eBay's completed auctions, and you'll be surprised not only at what people try to sell but also at what people will buy and how much they're willing to pay.

Deciding on a Particular Product

If you're considering a particular product or product line, do a search on eBay to see if that item or something similar is being offered for sale. In addition to checking active listings, look at the ended auctions to see what the final prices were for items that sold and how many didn't sell.

eBay has created a worldwide market that has driven prices down on many items that were previously hard to find but are now less so because of online auction sites. The law of supply and demand applies to eBay just as it does to any other selling venue.

If the market is saturated, decide whether you want to join the crowd or look for something else. Just because a lot of people are selling a particular item doesn't mean you shouldn't sell the same thing—especially if it's a popular, fast-moving product. However, you need to figure out if you're seeing a lot of listings for that product because it's popular and people are buying—or because the market is flooded and no one wants it. Also, keep in mind that in general, competition drives prices—and therefore profits—down. Study individual auctions for the bidding patterns to get an idea of the strength of the market.

What if no one else is offering the product for sale? That could mean that no one else has thought of it and you've got a wide-open market. Or it could mean that it's been tried and no one would buy. You might have to put it up for auction and see what happens.

Whatever you sell, you have to be able to sell enough of it to reach your income goals. For a steady income, you need steady supply sources. Hard-to-find collectible items will naturally have less competition than commonplace merchandise and typically sell for higher prices. Although they may be more profitable on a per-sale basis, you need to figure out if you can secure enough of them to do the sales volume you need.

"To make big money, you have to spend a lot of money; you've got to sell a lot of stuff," says Gary Hunt (eBay User ID: speedwind). "You've got to buy things right to be profitable."

What to Consider about Choosing a Product

No matter what you'd like to sell on eBay, there are certain issues common to every product that you should consider before making a decision.

Inventory Carrying Cost

The first issue to consider is the cost to carry the item. Let's say you paid $5 for an item and sold it for $25. Did you make a $20 profit? Not likely. That's why you need to calculate your inventory carrying cost.

The elements of inventory carrying cost include inventory financing charges or the opportunity cost of the inventory investment, insurance and taxes on inventory, material handling expenses, warehouse overhead, and inventory shrink, damage, and obsolescence. Calculating inventory carrying cost can be a sophisticated financial exercise, especially for large companies with huge inventories. For our purposes, we'll consider each element simply.

If you have to borrow money to purchase inventory, the interest you pay on that money is part of your carrying cost. If you use cash on hand to purchase inventory, you need to consider your opportunity cost, which is what that money could have been earning for you if it had been invested elsewhere.

Insurance and taxes on inventory should be fairly easy to calculate, but figuring out material handling expenses not directly associated with packing and shipping orders, as well as warehouse overhead, can be a little more complicated. When you're actually in business, you can estimate these costs. It will be difficult

WHAT YOU *CAN'T* SELL ON EBAY

Browse around eBay, and it looks as if just about anything and everything in the world is up for sale. But there are some restrictions on what you can sell on eBay, and you are responsible for making sure your items conform to eBay's guidelines.

Anything that is illegal or has the potential to harm or defraud someone is forbidden. For example, you are not allowed to sell human body parts—yours or anyone else's. A few years ago, one gutsy seller tried to auction one of his kidneys. As soon as eBay became aware of the listing, it was ended—but not before bidding reached $5.7 million.

Firearms and ammunition were also banned on eBay a few years ago, which created quite an uproar within the trading community and caused the National Rifle Association to issue a reproach. However, eBay's position was that as an online venue, it could not monitor or guarantee that buyers would meet all the qualifications (e.g., age restrictions, criminal records, and mental health history) and comply with laws that govern the sale of firearms. For basically the same reasons, alcohol, tobacco, and prescription drugs are also prohibited.

For the welfare of animals, eBay does not allow the sale of livestock or pets. This prevents unscrupulous breeders from having eBay as a venue to operate their unsavory businesses. Nor are you allowed to auction people, much to the sorrow of a disgruntled litigant who recently listed a Manhattan court housing judge for sale on eBay's site—she even included free worldwide shipping as a perk. But when eBay pulled the plug on the auction, the bids were only up to $127.

For more information on what you can and can't sell on eBay, check out the complete list of Prohibited and Restricted Items in eBay's Help section.

to forecast inventory shrink (theft), damage, and obsolescence until you have a track record, but you should assume that these situations will occur.

Storing and Shipping

You'll also need to consider the issues of physical storage and shipping. Do you have the room to keep the merchandise until it sells? How much does that space cost? Is it safe and secure?

Then there's the process and cost of packing and shipping. Even though most eBay buyers pay the actual shipping costs, there may still be labor and material expenses involved in the shipping process that come out of your profit.

Life Cycle

What is the product's life cycle? Is it a fad item like Beanie Babies? It's hard to predict when fads will run their course, but you want to avoid jumping in on the downside to avoid getting stuck with inventory you can't pay people to take from you. High-tech items often have a relatively short life cycle because of rapid technology advances. Pay attention to product life cycles so you can maximize your profits while the item is popular and move on to something else when the demand declines.

Where Do You Find Products?

Merchandise that you can sell for a profit is virtually everywhere. Garage and yard sales are still a great source of bargain-priced items that will sell on eBay. Estate sales organized by the family can also be great sources; those that are handled by professionals will generally not yield significant profits because the sale coordinators usually have a better idea of the value of what's in the estate than the average person trying to get his garage cleaned out. However, if you have access to a truck and storage space, you can buy the estates yourself, auction what you can on eBay, and sell the remainder through other channels. You can also find great deals at flea markets and thrift stores.

Offer to help local retailers get rid of their overstock by selling those items on eBay. You can either take the merchandise on consignment or buy it outright.

Clearance items at large chain stores may be priced low enough to enable you to sell them on eBay for a profit, especially if you buy at the end of the season and hold the merchandise until the following year. Kathy Logan (eBay User ID: rosie_peachstate) has stores she visits frequently for items she sells on eBay. "I call it 'checking my traps,'" she says. "I go to different places to see what's on sale and what the best deals are."

Shop going-out-of-business and bankruptcy sales. Watch for companies that are moving and need to get rid of inventory quickly. Whenever circumstances force a quick sale, the buyer benefits. Hunt gets most of his inventory by buying out the stock of independent hobby shops that are going out of business. Many small retailers in a range of industries are giving in to the competition from large chains and internet sales. When they go out of business, you can get a great deal on all or part of their inventory.

Use your imagination when thinking about who may have items you can sell. When part-time eBay seller Rhonda Haney (eBay User ID: 7713november) started selling on eBay, she specialized in memorabilia featuring French Canadian actor Roy Dupuis. She searched the internet for details on what magazines had articles and photographs of Dupuis, then shopped online sellers of used books and magazines to find those specific issues. She also contacted the publishers and requested copies of back issues. Buying the actual magazines was the easy part, she says. The real work was doing the research to find the publications in which he was featured. Once she had the magazines, she put them up for sale on eBay. One obsessed fan paid her $200 for a magazine that cost just a few dollars.

Then Haney contacted the photographers whose credits were listed in the articles on Dupuis and was able to sell prints of pictures of the actor that hadn't appeared in the publication. That same obsessed fan paid more than $1,000 for 50 black-and-white prints of Dupuis.

Haney figured out that these items would sell by searching for them on eBay and watching the prices. After about three years, Dupuis's U.S. popularity began to decline, and Haney started looking for another niche. Because she was only using eBay as a part-time opportunity to supplement her full-time job, Haney could survive the drop in online revenue.

When Hunt started selling on eBay, his vintage toy niche was too narrow. "I should have been more flexible in what I bought at the beginning, because if you're too narrow, there's only so much out there to buy," he says. "If you want to stay in business, you have to think ahead of how you are going to replace this merchandise that you are selling today."

Finally, don't forget your friends and family when looking for things to sell. Ask them to not donate or throw anything away until you've had a chance to evaluate it for selling on eBay. A survey conducted by ACNielsen revealed that American households have an average of $2,200 worth of unused items lying around—items that could be sold on eBay. Lisa Singer (eBay User ID: highend0) was taking clothes she didn't want anymore to a consignment shop. When she found out the consignment shop owner was selling those items on eBay, Singer decided to try putting up her own eBay auctions. She figured, why pay the consignment fee if she could sell on eBay herself? Once she got comfortable with the process, she started telling her friends—and offering to sell their high-end designer clothes. Before long, she had achieved Power Seller status and had a thriving eBay operation.

Always remember that eBay is a great source of items to sell on eBay. Many eBay sellers started as buyers and then accumulated so much stuff they began to resell their eBay purchases—recycling at its best. Also, you will find plenty of wholesale lots on eBay that you can buy and then split up and relist individually. Logan uses eBay as a source for quantity purchases that she resells. "It's just knowing what the current market value is and what people are going to need," she says.

As much as you may enjoy the process of shopping for your eBay inventory, it pays to streamline the process as much as possible. Not only is your time valuable, but the faster you find things, the more time you have to find and sell more things.

If you buy merchandise at thrift stores and garage sales, take a "hit and run" approach. When you know what you're looking for, you can be in and out in just a few minutes—and on to the next opportunity. Leisurely shopping is something you do for yourself or as a social outing with friends, not when you're buying for your business.

Wholesale Sources

Many high-volume eBay sellers buy from wholesale sources and sell those products on eBay at retail. While this can be profitable, it's important to choose your wholesaler wisely.

Don't waste your money buying lists of wholesalers. Such directories are available all over the internet and often only cost a few dollars, so it's tempting to take what seems to be a valid shortcut—but don't. You can get the same quality of information—or maybe even slightly better—for free by using any of the popular search engines. Just plug in keywords such as "wholesale," "manufacturers," or "drop-ship." The problem with this approach is that you still need to weed through thousands of companies to find one you'd like to do business with.

A better approach is to be more specific. First decide on the type of products you want to sell, then go looking for appropriate manufacturers, wholesalers, and distributors. Find companies whose products meet your quality expectations, that have prices and terms you can work with, and that deliver the service level you want to provide your customers. Ask for samples of the products so you can see the quality yourself. Some manufacturers and wholesalers send free samples, others charge a nominal fee. In any case, don't try to sell something you've never seen. Be sure it is truly worth what you expect to sell it for and that your customers will be satisfied with it. If it's not something you would buy for yourself, why would anyone else want to buy it from you?

Not every company that calls itself a wholesaler is truly a wholesaler. Do your homework to make sure you are really getting quality goods at wholesale prices.

Don't limit yourself to U.S.-based suppliers. You can also find plenty of high-quality goods at great prices from established overseas manufacturers. Importing is easier than ever, and it can be extremely profitable. In fact, thousands of eBay sellers are doing it. Deal with reputable companies, ask for references, and use a customs broker to help you deal with the import paperwork and duty. To get started buying from overseas suppliers, visit the U.S. Department of State's web site at www.state.gov. You'll find information about various countries, as well as links to the web sites of U.S. embassies and consulates, where staffers will be happy to help you with your international purchases.

Bob Bidwell (eBay User ID: plates-n-stuff) started his eBay business selling limited-edition collector plates. When he decided to expand to selling collectible action figures and model horses, he went to the manufacturers to build his own inventory. He told them exactly what he was doing and found they were happy to sell to him. "When I contacted them, I would tell them I was a homebased business without a storefront, which didn't seem to bother them," he says. "Because the internet is so big, a lot of the manufacturers realize that most of their collectible products are going to be sold online, not in a traditional mom-and-pop [brick-and-mortar] kind of store."

Be cautious about buying from liquidators. You might find some good deals, but more often, there's a good reason the product is being liquidated—and at least part of that reason is usually because no one wants it. Also, keep in mind that even though you'll find plenty of ads from companies billing themselves as liquidators, closeout sources, distributors, and wholesalers, so will anyone else who is considering these sources for merchandise.

Deal with the true manufacturer, wholesaler, or distributor—not a middleman who is marking up their prices and increasing your costs. Ask for references and talk to people who are buying from these suppliers. Then research the company itself; check with any industry associations, the consumer protection agency of the state in which the supplier is located, and any other source that may be able to give you information to help you make a purchasing decision.

That checking process is a two-way street. Legitimate manufacturers, wholesalers, and distributors will want information about you as well. Be prepared to prove that yours is a genuine business and that you have all necessary licenses and tax identification numbers. And be suspicious of any supplier who doesn't ask for this information. Also, avoid vendors who charge an account setup fee or any other fee, or who want to restrict what products you can sell. Legitimate companies make their money from selling their products, not from charging administrative fees.

Remember that you're able to set up shop on the internet for a small cash investment—scam artists can do the same thing. Don't become one of their victims.

Another important point to keep in mind about buying wholesale is that when you buy directly from a manufacturer, you are going to be dealing in volume. Most manufacturers have a minimum amount they will sell, and the more products you purchase, the better your cost per item will be. Before you make a wholesale purchase, be sure you have room to receive and store the inventory.

Drop-Shipping

On the surface, drop-shipping sounds like a great idea. Ideally, it works this way: You find a distributor of products you want to sell. You put photographs and a description of those products in your store site. When an order comes in, you process the payment (retail price plus shipping) and send the order to the distributor, who ships the product directly to your customer in a package that shows you as the shipper. The distributor bills you the wholesale price plus shipping and handling. You make a profit, the distributor makes a profit, the customer is happy and comes back for more.

Drop-shipping is a longstanding business practice, and when all parties involved do what they're supposed to, it's win-win. The distributor doesn't have to worry about the retail sales process; you don't have to stock inventory, handle the product, pack, ship, etc.

However, not all drop-shippers are created equal. Some do a great job, and some don't. When the product doesn't ship, the wrong item is shipped, it arrives damaged, or something else goes wrong, your customer doesn't care that the drop-shipper dropped the ball. He bought the product from you, and he expects you to deliver. If the drop-shipper doesn't deliver and you don't have any other way to get the merchandise, you'll have to issue a refund for the item and shipping costs, and you may not be able to recover that money from the drop-shipper. You will also lose your auction fees and—most importantly—your time. Check any drop-shipper's reputation thoroughly because yours depends on it. Make sure they have a solid track record, get references, and contact them.

Test your drop-shipper by placing an order and having it shipped to a friend so you can see what they ship and the condition it's in when it arrives. If there's a problem, you'll quickly see how the drop-shipper responds. Even when you have an ongoing relationship with a drop-shipper, periodically test them to be sure they are maintaining a high level of service.

Never use a drop-shipper unless you have actually seen the product to be sure the quality is acceptable. Some items might look great in photographs and turn out to be junk in your hands. If you find a great product through a drop-shipper, expect plenty of competition from other eBay sellers. Savvy sellers will quickly realize what you're doing and the company you're using, and they'll often jump on the bandwagon and flood the market. Be prepared to deal with this by staying constantly on the lookout for new products.

Another way to take advantage of the concept of drop-shipping and the service of a good drop-shipper is to use the drop-shipper to handle merchandise you already own. This saves you from having to do the physical part of storage and shipping. You arrange to have your inventory delivered to the drop-shipper's facility; the drop-shipper stores it for you; when you make a sale, you notify the drop-shipper what to ship and to whom. Find companies that will provide this type of service by searching under "fulfillment services."

Real-World Auctions

Auctions may also be a great source of inventory, but they require caution and self-discipline. Just about anything you can buy through other purchasing channels can be bought at auction. Deal only with reputable auction companies, know what you're buying, and be willing to walk away if someone bids higher than your top price.

Most auctions feature a carnival-like atmosphere, with vendors selling food and beverages, music blaring, and people milling about, reviewing their programs and examining the merchandise. When the auction actually begins, there will be a mad dash for seats. The adrenaline is flowing, because this is a competition unlike any other. The potential for profits is almost incalculable—but so is the possibility of losing your shirt.

Attend a few auctions without buying anything just to get the experience and learn how they operate. If you've ever gotten caught up in the excitement of a bidding war on eBay while sitting alone at your computer, you can only imagine what it must be like to be in a room full of people being egged on by a skilled auctioneer.

You'll find auctions advertised in national publications such as *USA Today* and *The Wall Street Journal*, as well as in local publications. To get on the bidders list so you receive announcements in the mail, send a written request to the auction company or government agency. Some web sites to visit to learn more about government auctions include the U.S. Treasury Department at www.treasury.gov/auctions/ and the federal government's official web portal at www.firstgov.gov/shopping/auctions/auctions.shtml. You might also check with your local city or county government or police agency to see if they hold auctions you may be interested in.

Plan to arrive at an auction at least an hour before the scheduled start time. That will give you time to get registered and to examine the merchandise that is up for sale. You may be required to show identification as part of the registration process, so be sure to have a driver's license or other legal ID with you. Find out ahead of time what payment methods will be accepted (for government auctions, it's usually cash or certified funds; some private auction companies may accept personal checks and/or credit cards).

As you check out what's for sale, look for things that would affect the item's resale potential, such as nicks, rips, scratches, missing parts, and fading. You should receive a catalog when you register, so make notes on it about items that catch your interest. You might also mark down the maximum you're willing to pay, and use that as a guide when the bidding begins.

You'll often find lots of assorted items—and combinations of treasures and trash—being auctioned. If you're bidding on one of these lots, make sure the items you are specifically interested in are still in the box when the bidding begins. Some auction attendees have been known to repack boxed lots to get a combination that they want. If you see one or two items in a lot that you want, check with one of the auction assistants to see if those pieces could be auctioned separately.

Keep in mind that it's easy to catch auction fever and bid more than an item is worth. One way to protect yourself is to bring someone you trust with you. Tell this person your game plan ahead of time, and when he or she nudges you and tells you to slow down or stop bidding, pay attention.

Become a Trading Assistant

Trading Assistants are experienced eBay sellers who sell items on eBay for people who, for whatever reason, don't want to do it themselves. There are plenty of people out there who have great things to sell, but are never going to take the time to post their items on eBay—and they're happy to pay a commission to someone who is willing to do it for them. These people can provide you with an endless source of items to sell.

As a Trading Assistant, you set up your own system for how you will deal with clients. You decide what services you'll provide, what types of merchandise you'll handle, the fees you'll charge, and all the other necessary terms.

Trading Assistant Jim Salvas (eBay User ID: camerajim) specializes in camera equipment and charges a commission of 20 to 40 percent, depending on the final sales value. Salvas absorbs the auction and payment processing fees in his commission, and guarantees that if he doesn't sell items within 14 days, he'll return them at no charge. Of course, he reserves the right to turn down consigned items if he feels they are not marketable on eBay. "I try to give people realistic expectations of what they can hope to sell their item for on eBay," he says. Other potential fee structures for Trading Assistants could include a flat or percentage listing fee in addition to the final value commission, whether or not the item sells.

eBay maintains a directory of Trading Assistants who have met the site's requirements. To qualify as a Trading Assistant, your eBay account must be in good standing, you must have sold at least four items within the past 30 days, and you must have a feedback score of 50 or higher, with 97 percent or more being positive.

eBay's Vehicle Listing Assistant program is similar to that of a Trading Assistant, but you would work with vehicle sales on eBay Motors. Listing Assistants provide data collection, photo services, listing creation, and inventory management. With the appropriate license (check with your state department of transportation), a Listing Assistant may also be able to provide complete end-to-end transaction services, including auction management, dealing with bidders, and post-sale processing.

While most of a Trading Assistant's clientele will be people who don't want to sell on eBay themselves, you may find some opportunities among other active eBay sellers. Some may have a line of products they want to sell that, for some reason, they don't want their name associated with. Others may not have time to personally handle everything they want to sell. For example, when Gary Hunt's vintage toy business grew big enough to require his full-time attention, he decided to hand his stamp business off to a Trading Assistant.

Set Up a Trading Post

A Trading Post is a store or other type of drop-off location operated by a highly experienced Trading Assistant. Clients can come by the Trading Post at their convenience during regular business hours without having to call ahead or schedule an appointment.

To qualify for the Trading Post designation, you must be a Trading Assistant with a feedback score of 500 or higher, 98 percent of it positive, and have sales of at least $25,000 on eBay each month.

It's common for successful Trading Assistants to want to open a Trading Post. Mack advises approaching that idea with caution. "By just taking what they are currently doing and putting it in a store, all they are doing is adding overhead," he says.

But Johnson says having a fixed location builds trust in your clientele. "People need to trust you to leave their high-end items with you," he says. "Brick-and-mortar has its advantages, even though it costs more." Johnson says a space of about 1,500 square feet would work for an eBay drop-off location. Your chances of success are much greater, he says, if you go with a franchise rather than starting on your own from scratch. In either case, expect to spend $75,000 to $100,000 in getting a retail operation up and running.

Of course, you don't need to qualify as a Trading Post to open a retail location that accepts items for sale on eBay. In fact, if you have a pawnshop, consignment store, or similar operation, eBay would make a great additional sales channel.

Mack uses eBay as an extra sales outlet for his chain of pawnshops. When store employees are not busy with onsite customers, they post items on eBay—and they get the same commission on sales, whether they take place online or in the store.

The services of a Trading Assistant or Trading Post allow sellers to remain anonymous—an issue that's important to some people. One Trading Post operator told us he regularly sells items brought in by a local golf pro who doesn't want it known that he's selling the expensive clubs, shoes, and other items manufacturers give him that he's not going to use.

Consignment Selling

Whether you become an actual Trading Assistant, open a Trading Post, or just get good enough that people ask you to sell for them, you should understand the issues involved in consignment selling on eBay. Selling on consignment means the owner of the item asks you to handle the sale process and pays you for your efforts. When the item is sold and delivered, you deduct your fees and commission from the sale price and send your client a check for the remainder.

Consignment fees can range from as low as 10 percent to as high as 30 percent or more. Never accept anything on consignment without a written contract spelling out all your terms and conditions. Keep in mind that the seller may have an inflated perception of the value of the merchandise due to emotional attach-ment; part of your job is to tactfully let him know how much he can realistically expect to get—but, of course, make no guarantees.

Always take physical possession of items you are auctioning on consignment. Even though you are not the actual seller, Salvas says, "You are putting your repu-tation as a seller on the line. It's important to take possession of the merchandise and take care of the shipping and everything else. Otherwise, a lot of things could go wrong." For example, a seller asking you to handle a consignment item may want you to do the eBay part and promises to handle the shipping. But if the seller doesn't ship, perhaps because he wasn't happy with the amount the item sold for, or if he ships but packages the item so poorly that it arrives damaged, you're the one who will have to deal with the resulting customer service issues. Better to han-dle it yourself and know that it will be done right.

Bargain to Get Bargains

It makes perfect sense: when you're buying, you want to pay the lowest possible price—and when you're selling, you want the buyer to pay the highest possible price.

When you're selling on eBay, there's no real negotiation involved. You decide on the minimum you'll accept, and the person who bids the highest amount above that gets the item.

However, when you're buying merchandise to sell on eBay, your negotiation skills can mean the difference between a profit and a loss. Start by knowing the mar-ket value of the products you intend to sell before you buy them, then figure out the maximum that you can pay for the products and still make the profit you want. If you can't get the merchandise for that amount or less, walk away from the deal.

Whether your supplier is an individual, a small company, or a huge corpora-tion, find out if the price is negotiable. The easiest way to do that is to simply ask. If the merchandise price is firm, you still might be able to deal on payment terms, shipping costs, delivery arrangements, or any other aspect of the transaction.

Your initial offer should be fair and reasonable—but always less than the asking price. You can always increase your offer, but you can't reduce it once the number is on the table. When you make your offer, explain it in a way that won't offend the seller. For example, let's say you're at a garage sale and the seller is asking $150 for a lot of vintage jewelry. Some of it is junk, but there are several pieces that you know will sell at a decent price.

Don't say, "You want $150 for this? There's no way this stuff is worth more than $75." That insults the seller's intelligence and taste—after all, that could be a beloved grandmother's jewelry that you've maligned while at the same time telling the seller that he doesn't know how to price things.

You could say, "I'll give you $75 for it," and see what the seller does. Chances are, she'll either stick to the marked price or counteroffer—but it's not likely she'll say, "Okay, I'll take it."

But if you say, "You've got some nice pieces in this lot, and I understand why you feel it's worth $150. However, considering the market and what it's going to take for me to resell it, I can only offer you $75."

Then be quiet and wait for a response. Whenever you make an offer to buy something, don't say anything else until the seller responds—no matter how long the silence lasts or how uncomfortable you feel.

When you get a response, react appropriately. For example, if the seller accepts your offer, close the deal. If he turns it down, continue negotiating until you are absolutely certain he will not accept your maximum price.

Another approach is to not make an offer, but instead let the seller name a lower price. Simply ask, "What is the lowest amount you'll take for this?" You'll get one of three responses.

Using our vintage jewelry example, the seller may say, "It's marked at $150, and that's what I want for it." You can respond with a lower offer, you can decide it's worth the asking amount, or you can walk away.

Or the seller may say, "I'd like to get at least $100." Now you have a new starting point for your negotiations. Or the seller may name a price that is actually lower than what you were willing to pay—a bonus for you.

A third response you'll commonly get is, "What will you give me for it?" You can either try to get the seller to say a number, or you can make an offer to get the negotiations started.

Regardless of what you're buying or whom you're buying it from, always treat everyone with respect, listen to the other person's point of view, be fair and reasonable, and work to reach a win-win solution.

Buying Tips

Smart buying can increase your profits substantially; buying mistakes can cost you dearly. Keep the following tips in mind.

- *Know your seller.* Be sure you're buying from someone you can trust to operate with integrity and ethics. When you buy luxury items such as designer clothes and high-end jewelry to resell on eBay, ask to see the seller's driver's license and make a copy of it for your files.

- *Leave a paper trail.* If you buy from individuals and there is even the remotest chance that anyone might question the veracity of the items, have the seller sign a bill of sale that clearly describes the goods involved. If the seller balks, reconsider your buying decision. Should it turn out that the merchandise has been stolen, having a bill of sale may protect you from criminal prosecution. Companies should provide appropriate documentation automatically; if they don't, reconsider your buying decision.

- *Buy generic and off-brand items cautiously.* Selling brand names is likely to be easier and more profitable than off-brands. Whether the product is new or used, most people prefer to buy brands they recognize and trust.

- *Go for a trial run.* Before making a long-term commitment to a drop-shipper or buying from a wholesaler, complete a sample purchase so you can see how they operate.

- *Go to the source.* Contact the actual manufacturer of products you want to sell to see if you can buy direct. Not all manufacturers will sell direct, even in large quantities; many will only go through authorized distributors. But the closer you can get to the source, the fewer markups you'll have to pay.

CHAPTER 6

The Tools of Your eBay Trade

ETTING SET UP AS AN EBAY SELLER is easy. Building a substantial, profitable business using eBay as a selling platform takes a bit more work. With the appropriate tools, you can create a professional online image that inspires confidence in buyers. You can also automate your operation for increased efficiency and profitability, and deliver topnotch service that will keep customers coming back.

eBay Tools

eBay provides users with a wide range of buying and selling tools and is constantly improving those tools and developing new ones. The goal is to make your eBay business as efficient and profitable as possible—after all, the easier it is for you to sell and make money on eBay, the more you will do it. The more you do it, the bigger eBay grows. The bigger eBay grows, the bigger your market becomes. It's an exciting, positive, upward spiral, and it's easy for you to take advantage of that momentum.

My eBay

This automatic tool is available to all registered eBay users. My eBay is a central place where you can track and manage all your eBay buying, selling, messaging, account information, preferences, and more. My eBay information is private and available only to the user. You can easily customize this tool to suit the way you do business on eBay.

For buyers, My eBay provides a central place to monitor items they are either watching or bidding on, to track auctions they did and didn't win, to pay for and leave feedback on closed auctions, and to keep information on their favorite searches, sellers, and categories.

Sellers can use My eBay to monitor current auctions (as well as those scheduled to be launched), invoice buyers, print shipping labels, make a second chance offer, sell a similar item, relist an unsold item, and more. For small- to medium-volume sellers, My eBay will efficiently manage all operations, from listing to leaving feedback.

Turbo Lister

This free tool is rich in features for medium- to high-volume sellers. It creates auction listings in bulk, provides free, easy-to-use HTML templates, allows you to schedule when auctions should be launched, lets you make bulk edits to multiple listings at one time, and allows you to save and duplicate listing details so you can reuse them when creating listings for similar auctions.

Turbo Lister is easier and faster to use when preparing multiple auctions than eBay's Sell Your Item form. It can even be used in conjunction with other auction management software, such as Seller's Assistant or a non-eBay management system.

Seller's Assistant

Medium- and high-volume sellers may want to consider eBay's Seller's Assistant. For a monthly fee, you can use this tool to create and list auctions in bulk, track and manage active auctions, send automated personalized e-mails to customers, leave feedback in bulk, create shipping labels, and process invoices. Seller's Assistant stores closed listings and sales records on your own computer. The basic version is recommended for medium-volume sellers; high-volume sellers should consider the pro version. Seller's Assistant is accessed through your desktop and requires a download to your hard drive.

Selling Manager

This organizational tool is accessible through your My eBay and is available for a small monthly subscription fee. It helps to keep track of your auctions once they have been listed, as well as advise you of post-closing activities that need to be completed. There are customized templates for e-mail and feedback, and you can print shipping labels and send invoices with just a click. In addition to the basic version, there is also a pro version for high-volume sellers that helps manage inventory, provides selling statistics, and offers free designer templates. This program works well with the Seller's Assistant. Selling Manager Pro is available for free to Featured and Anchored Store sellers.

Seller's Assistant and Selling Manager can be used independently or together—and combined with Turbo Lister for optimum results. Use the feature comparison table located in eBay's Seller Tools section to help you decide what's best for your particular operation.

Shipping Calculator

Use eBay's free shipping calculator page to determine accurate domestic and international rates for shipping via USPS and UPS. The shipping calculator lets you add handling fees so your customers see one total. You can also include a shipping calculator box in your auction pages for domestic bidders. When a buyer checks out, the rates are automatically added to the invoice based on the destination zip code.

Tools Wizard

Confused by all the choices on eBay? That's understandable—and it's why eBay has created the Tools Wizard to help you decide what tools are most appropriate for your type of business. The Wizard takes you through a series of questions, then suggests one or more tools and provides a link to more information. Go to Seller Tools, then click on Tool Recommendations to find the Tools Wizard.

Solutions Directory

Got a question or a problem? Are you doing something that you think could be improved? Check out the eBay Solutions Directory, an online information bank with services and software from eBay and compatible third-party providers.

Buyer/Bidder Management

One of the most valuable benefits of selling on eBay is getting your products in front of millions of potential customers, but there may be times when you want to control who can bid on your auctions. One way to do that is to create a blocked bidder/buyer list. When you add a User ID to this list, that person will not be able to bid on or purchase any of the items you have up for any type of auction. Consider using this tool when you have had a bad experience with a bidder (including non-paying, slow-paying, or unreasonably demanding bidders), and simply don't want to do business with that person again. Of course, this tool may limit the number of bids on your auctions—but it can also reduce your problems if your items seem to attract bidders you don't want to deal with.

eBay's other bidder management tool is the preapproved bidder/buyer list, which you can create to allow only specified users to bid on a particular auction. If a user not on your preapproved list tries to place a bid, he will be asked to contact you by e-mail. You can add or remove bidders from your pre-approved list until the auction ends.

The preapproved list tool is useful when you want to sell something to a particular bidder but do not want to open the auction up to the public. Let's say you put an item up with a starting bid of $59; no one bid on it, so it closed without a sale. But after the auction ends, you receive an e-mail offering you $50 for the item, and you decide to accept. It's against eBay policies to complete the sale outside eBay. The easiest and most efficient way to handle the situation is for you to relist the item with a $50 starting bid and create a preapproved bidder list that includes only the User ID of the bidder you have agreed to sell to.

PayPal

In addition to being an eBay subsidiary and the site's preferred payment method, PayPal offers sellers a number of free auction and reporting tools that expedite the handling of the post-auction tasks. PayPal's Post-Sale Manager monitors payments, invoices, feedback, and shipments. You can set your account to automatically insert the PayPal logo in all your listings, which lets your customers know they can pay easily and safely through their bank account or credit card. PayPal's Shipping Center is integrated with the USPS and UPS, and lets you calculate rates, print labels, track shipments, and more.

Like eBay, PayPal regularly adds and improves services, so periodically browse through the site to see what's new that you can use.

Third-Party Tools

eBay's impressive growth has spawned a substantial market for third-party software and other online auction management tools. Some can be purchased outright; others are available for a monthly subscription fee; and still others are free for the taking. You'll find many third-party products listed in eBay's solutions directory, or you can search the internet yourself to find providers. Third-party software is particularly useful if you'll be selling on auction sites other than eBay. Here is just a sample of what's available to help you manage your online business:

Auction Management Tools

These are some tools that can help streamline and effectively manage your online auctions.

ALL MY AUCTIONS (WWW.RAJEWARE.COM)
This software tracks your auctions and compiles reports to your specifications. The program includes an auction calculator, as well as templates for e-mails, shipping labels, and packing slips.

ANDALE (WWW.ANDALE.COM)
Use one of Andale's free counters to track how many times your listings are viewed. Andale also offers a range of research, auction, store, and management tools at competitive prices.

AUCTION SUBMIT SOFTWARE (WWW.AUCTIONSUBMIT.COM)
This free software allows you to submit auctions to multiple sites and performs a range of auction management functions. The vendor offers this product free in the hope that you might purchase additional programs.

MARKET WORKS (WWW.AUCTIONWORKS.COM)
Formerly known as Auction Works, this is a leading provider of comprehensive online marketplace management software and services.

VIEWTRACKER (WWW.SELLATHON.COM)
This popular tracking software tells you exactly how your auction visitors found you, what keywords they searched for, what categories they browsed, how they sorted their search results, whether they're watching your auction, if they're planning a snipe, and more.

SHOOTING STAR (WWW.FOODOGSOFTWARE.COM)
This affordably priced program uses a workflow system to help manage your auctions. It tracks your auctions and lets you know what you need to do, and when.

THE POSTER TOASTER (WWW.THEPOSTERTOASTER.COM)
A free bulk listing tool that is, as the name implies, as "easy as toast."

Free Auction Templates

Use auction templates to generate attractive listings easily and quickly. After you enter the appropriate information, the template converts your text to HTML that you can copy and paste in eBay's listing description form. The sites listed here offer free templates plus a range of other free and fee-based services for online sellers.

AUCTION MOMS (WWW.AUCTIONMOMS.COM)
An excellent resource for beginners, this site features free auction templates that are easy to use, as well as other tools, tips, and resources.

AUCTION RICHES (WWW.AUCTIONRICHES.COM)
This is a membership site with a range of services, but it does offer a free basic ad creator (the link is on the home page) that uses simple colored borders and backgrounds.

AUCTION SUPPLIES (WWW.AUCTIONSUPPLIES.COM)
Once you've gained some experience with HTML, you'll find the templates on this site interesting.

NUCITE (WWW.NUCITE.COM)
Nucite's selection of free templates is limited, but the quality is excellent. The site has a number of other auction management services worth checking out.

Miscellaneous Tools

SPEED TYPING (WWW.COLORPILOT.COM)
This free program available through Color Pilot (which also has a selection of fee-based software tools) allows you to store frequently used phrases and paragraphs so you can drop them into your text (e-mails or auction descriptions) by entering a keyword. For example, if you have a standard paragraph describing your shipping terms, Speed Typing will place that text where designated when you type a keyword such as "ship." Georgene Harkness (eBay User ID: mynewthreads) uses this tool in both auction descriptions and e-mails. "I have a standard note that I send out to people with mailing instructions, and all I have to do is type in a keyword and there's my note."

THANK-YOU NOTES (WWW.ETHICAL2004.COM)
Make a great impression on people who bid on your auctions—even though they didn't win—by sending every bidder a thank-you note. A tool that will send every bidder one thank-you note (recognizing that many bidders bid more than once) is available through Ethical Technologies.

JPEG MAGIC (WWW.JPEGMAGIC.COM)
This image optimizer and compressor tool has an easy interface for rotating, lightening, and darkening photos. "The best part is that it compresses large images while retaining the quality of the photo," Harkness says. "People on dial-up don't get tired of waiting for the picture to download."

ONLINE POSTAGE
High-volume USPS users can use www.stamps.com and www.endicia.com to purchase postage, print labels, and track shipments online.

Arm Yourself

In the early days of World War II, Winston Churchill said, "Give us the tools, and we will finish the job." As an eBay seller, you have all the tools you need—and then some. In fact, you may find your choices overwhelming. To cope, don't explore too many different options at once—and resist the urge to purchase the entire set of fireworks when all you really need to shine is a box of sparklers. Take advantage of free software or the free trial periods that many vendors offer. In the absence of a trial period, find out what sort of satisfaction and performance guarantee is included before you spend any money. And visit the discussion forums on eBay and through other channels to see what other sellers have to say about various tools.

eBay is working hard to create new tools to make it easier and more efficient for both buyers and sellers. At the same time, third-party vendors are developing products for eBay and other online auctions and sales sites. "There is a collision of great stuff going on," says Steve Mack (eBay User ID: ztradingpost). He says over the next few years, the market will shake out the marginal products and leave the best technology—fewer choices, but better products for even greater online success.

CHAPTER 7

Great Listings Are the Foundation of Selling on eBay

THERE IS NO SINGLE KEY TO SUCCESS when it comes to selling on eBay, but putting together great listings is extremely important. Your auction listings need to create desire, inspire confidence, and move people to transition from browser to bidder. You should apply these fundamentals of great listings to your nonauction items as well.

Keep in mind that there are two sides to eBay's phenomenal success. You may have a worldwide market of millions of people for your eBay business—but so do millions of other eBay sellers. You'll have more potential customers, but also more competition. That's why you need to put together auctions that stand out and are findable through whatever search techniques your customers are likely to use.

Choose Your Auction Format

The classic eBay auction format is referred to as an online auction. Its appeal is its simplicity: you post your item with a starting bid, then sit back and wait for bidders to compete with each other for the privilege of buying your merchandise.

It's a good way to start and a fun way to buy, but it's not your only option. Depending on what you're selling and your overall business strategy, you may want to use other auction formats.

Buy It Now (BIN)

By adding this feature to a standard auction, you can give bidders the option to either bid on your product or buy it immediately. The BIN price is typically higher than your opening bid, but still in the fair market range. When a bidder agrees to the BIN price, the auction ends. If someone places a bid below the BIN price, the option disappears.

Here's how it works: You have a pair of binoculars to sell with a manufacturer's suggested retail price of $129. Most of the discount stores sell that item for around $100. You post the binoculars with a starting bid of $9.99 and a BIN price of $49.99. If the first bidder is willing to pay $49.99 and clicks on the BIN price, the auction ends and the sale is made. If the first bidder wants to take a chance and see if he can get the binoculars for less than $49.99, he bids $9.99, the BIN option disappears, and the auction proceeds as any other auction. The binoculars might go for $9.99—or the auction might end with a much higher sale price, sometimes even higher than the original BIN or even the fair market value.

A popular strategy is to set your starting bid amount for the absolute minimum you're willing to sell the item for, and the BIN amount at close to full retail. If you get anything in-between, you've made a profit and the customer has gotten a good deal.

Reserve Price

Reserve-price auctions have a hidden minimum price that is the lowest amount the seller is willing to accept. Sellers can start the bidding below the reserve amount, but are not obligated to sell the item if the reserve is not met. Buyers are not shown what the reserve price is; they only see that there is one and whether or not it has been met.

If the auction closes and the reserve is not met, the seller has the option to offer the item to any one of the nonwinning bidders through a Second Chance Offer with a Buy It Now price equal to each bidder's maximum bid. For example, if you set a reserve price of $25 and your highest bid is $23, you are not obligated to sell the item at all—but if you want to, you can offer it to the person who bid $23 for that amount.

Some sellers see reserve pricing as a way to protect their investment without revealing upfront how much they want to get for the item. At the same time, many bidders avoid reserve auctions because they can't tell what the lowest winning bid needs to be, and they don't want to waste their time placing bids if they don't have a chance of winning the item.

Fixed Price

A fixed-price listing is actually not an auction but it comes up on auction search results. It's used to sell items at a set price, much like a traditional retail sale, usually by sellers who have multiples of commodity items. The sale is immediate; there's no bidding or waiting.

For example, let's say you got a great deal on a wholesale lot of 25 identical stuffed toy dogs. You paid $2 each for them, and you're willing to sell them for $5.99 (plus shipping and handling). You can put up a single fixed-price listing showing the 25 toys available for $5.99 each, and buyers can purchase whatever amount they want, up to the number you have, without waiting for the auction to end. You save time and money by putting up just one listing instead of 25 separate auctions.

Dutch (or Multiple Item) Auction

This vehicle for selling two or more identical items in the same auction is perhaps the most interesting—and complicated—auction format. You decide on your minimum bid amount, and bidders specify the number of items they want and the highest price per item they're willing to pay. When the auction closes, all the winning bidders pay the same price per item, which is the lowest successful bid.

Here's what a Dutch auction for those 25 stuffed toy dogs might look like: You put them up with a starting bid of $5.50 each. If you got 25 bidders, all wanting only one dog, for $5.50 each, then that's what you'd sell them for. But let's say one person bid $6 for 15 and another person bid $7 for 10. You would sell them all for

$6, which is the lowest successful bid. That means the person who bid $7 would actually get the toys for $6 each.

Of course, Dutch auctions aren't always that simple. For the final price to be more than the starting bid, all the winning bidders have to bid more than the starting amount. If, for example, you had three bidders—one bid on 10 toys at $6 each, another bid on 10 toys at $7 each, and a third bid on 5 toys at $5.50 each—all 25 would be sold for $5.50 each.

What if you have more bids than product? Start counting back from the highest bid until you reach the number of bids that matches the number of items; then everyone pays that bid price. That would look like this: Bidder A bid on 15 of the toys for $5.50 each; Bidder B bid on 5 for $6 each; and Bidder C bid on 10 for $5.75 each. All the toys will be sold for $5.50 each. Bidder A will get his 15; Bidder B will get his 5; and there are 5 left for Bidder C, who can accept half as many as he wanted for $5.50, which is less than what he was willing to pay, or he can refuse them. In a Dutch auction, a winning bidder has the right to refuse partial quantities if he wins some, but not all, of the items he bid on.

In most cases, all bidders in a Dutch auction end up paying the starting price. Bidders do not receive outbid notices from eBay, nor can they use eBay's proxy bidding system. All items in a single Dutch auction must be absolutely identical, and the auction must be listed in the appropriate category.

For both Dutch (multi-item) auction listings and fixed-price listings, the price times the quantity must be less than $100,000.

Private Auction

This format lets your bidders remain anonymous. In most auction formats, anyone looking at the item can see the User IDs of all the bidders. In a private auction, the bidders' IDs are not seen on the item or bidding history screens; when the auction is over, only the seller and winning bidder are notified via e-mail.

This format is useful when you believe your prospective bidders may not want their identities disclosed to the general public. For example, when a well-known collector is bidding on an item, that knowledge can greatly increase the interest in the auction and drive the price up—which is good for the seller, but not the buyer. For this reason, it's common for these collectors to prefer private auctions to prevent their bids from being monitored. Private auctions are also appropriate when the item is sensitive in nature, such as adult material.

However, the foundation of eBay is its openness, so only use the private auction format when there is a valid reason for it.

Restricted-Access Auction

To make it easy for buyers and sellers to find or avoid adult-only merchandise, eBay offers a Mature Audiences area for material not appropriate for viewing by minors. Check eBay's site for complete details on what can and can't be sold in this area, and how to access it.

Set Your Price

Traditional retailers buy stock, mark it up according to whatever fair and reasonable formula they prefer to use, and put it out for sale. You can use the same approach when you put stock in an eBay store or post fixed-price listings. But in an auction, the buyer determines the final selling price—and that makes maintaining your desired level of profitability a challenge.

The first step in profitable pricing is to know the value of what you're selling. Even if all you want to do is clear out your closets, you'll stand a better chance of getting the best possible price if you know the market value of what you're selling. If your goal is building a profitable business, understanding value is critical.

A great way to find out what things are selling for on the internet is to conduct a Froogle search (www.froogle.com). Froogle was created by the popular search engine Google to search shopping sites for specific items. Search results show the item, price, a photo if available, and a link to the purchase site. The number of links the search request produces will give you an idea of how popular the product is. You should also check out standard retail outlets for competitive pricing information.

Although it helps to know what items are selling for in the general market outside eBay, it does not necessarily mean that's what people will pay on eBay. Search the site for completed auctions of similar items; study the bid patterns and winning bids. Consider what your costs are, and decide if there is sufficient potential profit in what you want to sell. If so, move forward. If not, go back to your plan and revise.

Starting Price Strategies

Your starting price, or opening bid, is the absolute minimum you'll take for an item (unless you have set a reserve price). Many eBay sellers set their starting bid low—often way below the actual value or their cost—and trust the market to drive the price up to a profitable level. You'll often see items worth hundreds—sometimes even thousands—of dollars starting at 99 cents with no reserve, but closing near or even above the retail value. Just remember: if you use this strategy, you have to be prepared to take the loss if the auction closes with a winning bid that is below your cost.

The 99-cent starting bid works best when you have a large potential market and are likely to attract a number of bidders competing for a good deal. If your market is narrow, the strategy may not work for you. For example, Nona Van Deusen (eBay User ID: stylebug.com) is reluctant to try a 99-cent starting price for her high-end designer clothes. "The woman has got to fit into the gown, so that narrows the market," she says. "Say you have a size six Badgley Mischka gown, but perhaps in that ten-day period [of the auction], there is only one size-six person interested in that color gown." You could easily have a gown that retails for $3,000 or more selling for less than a dollar.

Another strategy is to start your pricing at or just a few dollars above your cost. While this assures that you won't lose money on the sale, you might miss out on some bidders. Most eBay shoppers are looking for bargains and are put off by a higher starting bid. Often a lower starting bid will generate enough interest to prompt a bidding war, which will drive the final price up. Also, many buyers search by starting price, so the lower your opening bid, the better your chances of showing up prominently in those search results.

Karen Kelley (eBay User ID: thepinkboutique) says that she knows clothing labels, and what sells and what doesn't. She says, "I always start an item at least double, sometimes triple, what I invested in it. The exception to that are couture items which are going to sell for a lot more."

Gary Neubert (eBay User ID: gatorpack) uses two primary criteria to establish prices. "We have margin targets and we look at the competitiveness of our prices," he says. "We try to maintain a balance between those two areas. We are not going to be the lowest priced and we are not going to be the highest priced. But the most important criteria is maintaining our margin objectives."

Neubert believes a common reason eBay sellers fail is pricing errors. "A seller who is going to be successful on eBay has to be able to buy their product right," he says. "You have to be able to consider all of your costs, and price your item accordingly. Do not rely on the auction proxy-bidding mechanism to set the price for you. Otherwise, you will run out of money or go into debt and have to close up shop." This means researching your product's profitability and knowing in advance what the market demand is for it.

eBAY FEES

eBay fees are how the site generates revenue to operate. Consider them the equivalent of rent for in a retail location. Check the eBay site for current rates. eBay Motors and real estate fees are structured differently than standard auctions. The following are the basic auction fees you can expect to pay:

- *Insertion fee.* This fee is the cost to put your listing on eBay. It's based on the opening bid or reserve price you have set for your item and is not refundable. For most auctions, the insertion fee ranges from 30 cents to $4.80.

- *Final value fee.* When your item sells, you are charged a final value fee that is a percentage of the closing price. The final value fee starts at 5.25 percent and decreases as the closing price increases. If your item does not sell, you do not pay a final value fee. If your item sells but the winning bidder doesn't pay, you can apply for a refund of your final value fee.

- *Optional feature fees.* Beyond the basic features, you can purchase optional features including reserve price, listing upgrades, photo services, and seller tools. These features and the current related fees are outlined on eBay.

Ron and Sheri Walker (eBay User ID: beansantiques) invest a significant amount of time researching their vintage products to determine accurate market values. Once they bought a small metal cross that looked like a piece of scrap iron that Ron figured wasn't even worth $10. But he researched it and found out that it was part of a Zeppelin that had been shot down in World War I. "The man who shot it down extracted 12 pieces of metal from the Zeppelin, signed each one, and gave them to his friends," Ron says. "This was one of the original 12 and it sold for more than $1,000. Research is a big, big thing."

In Addition to Starting Price

You may just set your starting price and let the auction go. Or you might want to add a Buy It Now price to give a bidder the opportunity to make an immediate purchase. Or you might add a reserve price to make sure you get the final amount you want.

Attention-Grabbing Auction Titles

You have 45 characters (letters and spaces) for your listing's title, so make each one count. Your title should make a prospective bidder want to learn more about your auction.

Clever and catchy titles are good, but what's more important is that the title be clear, accurate, and factual. Tricking people into looking at your auction because they think it's something else won't get you more bids—but it will annoy people who are likely to remember that trick the next time they look at one of your auctions. Also, misleading titles are against eBay's policy and could result in your auction being ended early.

eBay suggests using descriptive keywords that clearly convey what you're selling. Include the brand name, artist, or designer, and state exactly what the item is, even if the title repeats the category name. Get ideas by browsing closed listings for similar items and see which titles drew high closing prices. Keep in mind that many buyers don't check "search title and description," so include the primary words your prospective buyers might use to search for your item.

Auction titles with accurate keywords are critical. "There are millions of things listed every day that people have to wade through," says Ron Walker. "You may have the crown jewels to sell, but if you don't put the right words in the title, no one will see them. If you're unable to title it, you will be unable to sell it."

You might see things like "L@@K," "Nice," "Wow!" and other generic adjectives in titles, but these elements do not attract additional bidders. Consider that buyers don't search on these terms, so they're a waste of your valuable space. Also, to an experienced eBayer, such words in a title brand you as an amateur—not the image you want to project.

For a small extra fee, you can add a subtitle to your listing to provide additional descriptive information below the main title that buyers will see when browsing categories or viewing search results. However, any keywords in your subtitle will not be picked up by the search unless the buyer has checked the "search title and description" box, so don't depend on a subtitle to serve as a keyword search tool. The details in the subtitle are designed to encourage the buyer to open your listing once they've found it.

Irresistible Descriptions

Once you've grabbed a shopper's attention with your title, give her what she's looking for with a fabulous description. A well-crafted description gives bidders the information they need to make a buying decision: It demonstrates that you are a professional, conscientious seller and pays off in the final sale price.

Be clear, complete, and concise. Use powerful, persuasive words. Sloppy, incomplete, or vague descriptions make bidders leery of doing business with you. Don't assume that your buyers know anything about your item; tell them everything they need to know to make a bidding decision. Though you should always include at least one photograph of your item, write your description as if you have no pictures, because you never know when something might go wrong and the image won't display.

Your description should include

- the name of the item, even though it repeats the title.
- what the item is made of.
- when and where it was made.
- who made it (manufacturer, artist, designer, author, etc.).
- the condition (new, like new, used, damaged, etc.).

- weight, size, and/or dimensions.
- notable features or markings.
- any special background or history.
- suggestions for using the item.

Bidders can e-mail you using a link on your listing page if they want more information, but don't assume that they will. Some will ask; others will simply move on to bid on an item with a better description.

Build a personal reference library with books and resources about your product, and use that information to write thorough descriptions. Gary Hunt (eBay User ID: speedwind) estimates that he owns 1,000 reference books on toys and collectibles. "You have to know about what you're selling," he says. "People put up 'old toy truck.' Who is going to even find it, much less have any confidence that you know what you're talking about?" But, he says, if you use the brand name and specifics, including a model number, type of truck, condition, year made, size, etc., then it's obvious you know your products. "People will spend $5,000 a year buying old toys, but they won't spend $25 to buy a book. If you've got the book, you can study your field, learn what things are worth, and do a better job describing your items." Especially when it comes to collectibles, the more specific your title and description, the greater the number of people who will be interested in bidding on it.

Make the tone of your description warm and friendly. "You've got to make it sound like you really want somebody's business, and that you're excited and you're not spending 90 percent of your energy thinking about the one percent of things that could go wrong," Hunt says. If you've used the item yourself, explain the benefits and why you like—or don't like—it. Make suggestions for how the item might be used by a buyer. Don't try to hide any flaws; your customer will find out when the product arrives anyway. So be upfront about the item's condition.

Use words that sell. Strong adjectives and powerful action words will support your photographs and enhance the appeal of your listing.

If appropriate, use the element of scarcity. Is your item rare? A limited edition? Will it still be available next month or next year? Is the price likely to go up in the future? Tap into the bidder's fear that if he doesn't win this item right now, he'll never have another chance to acquire it—and certainly not at this price.

ALPHABET SOUP

Learn the eBay lingo. Here are the common abbreviations you'll see and use in eBay titles and item descriptions:

COA: Certificate of authenticity

DJ: Dust jacket (for hardcover books)

FE: First edition

FS: Factory sealed

HB: Hardback book

HTF: Hard to find

MIB: Mint (meaning in perfect condition) in box

MIJ: Made in Japan

MIMB: Mint in mint box (meaning both the item and the box are in mint condition)

MIP: Mint in package

MNB: Mint no box

MOC: Mint on card

MOMC: Mint on mint card

MONMC: Mint on near mint card

MWBT: Mint with both tags

MWMT: Mint with mint tags

NARU: Not a registered user (suspended eBay user)

NBW: Never been worn

NC: No cover

NIB: New in box

NIP: New in package

NM: Near mint

NR: No reserve (meaning there is no reserve price on the auction)

NRFB: Never removed from box

NW: Never worn

NWT: New with tags

NWOT: New without tags

OOP: Out of print

PB: Paperback

RET: Retired

SH/S&H: Shipping and handling

VHTF: Very hard to find

You've probably seen television advertisements for specially minted collector coins that end with the phrase "Only five sets per household, please" or something similar. Many buyers who might have bought only one or two sets will be prompted to buy five because they believe it's all they can get. Use this technique, or be more creative. If appropriate and accurate, you can blame weather conditions, labor strikes, or other factors, or just say you don't know when you'll "get another shipment at this price."

When you're finished, proofread and spell-check—and then proofread again. Use the checklist in Figure 7.1 as a guide.

FIGURE 7.1: **LISTING CHECKLIST**

❏ Select your auction format.

❏ Select your category.

❏ Set your price.

❏ Write your title.

❏ Write your description.

❏ State your policies (payment, shipment, returns, etc.).

❏ Take a great photograph.

❏ Determine your timing (length of auction, start and end day and time).

❏ Choose a template or write HTML code.

❏ Launch your auction.

❏ Monitor your e-mail, and answer questions promptly.

In Addition to the Item Description, Include . . .

Your listing should also include details that will help bidders decide if they want to do business with you. Be sure to clearly state your shipping rates, schedule, and policies (including what carriers you use, whether or not you require insurance, what options you offer your customers, etc.). Also include your return and refund policy and acceptable payment methods. "You have to make your rules very clear," says Lisa Singer (eBay User ID: highend0). And even then, she adds, people will bid without reading your policies and then complain because they don't like the way you operate.

Seth Schmidt (eBay User ID: shutterbladestore) leaves nothing to chance by including the following in his auction descriptions:

Why Buy from Us?

1. Our products are covered by a 10-day inspection period and 30-day warranty.

2. We are an eBay Powerseller with a 99+ percent positive feedback rating.

3. We have thousands of satisfied eBay customers.

4. What you see is what you get—our pictures are of the actual item you are bidding on.

5. We ship promptly via UPS—within one to two business days (Monday through Friday) of your payment.

6. We professionally package your item for safe shipment.

7. We insure every package we ship.

8. We answer your e-mails promptly Monday through Friday, 9:00 A.M. to 6:00 P.M. EST. (We do not answer e-mail over the weekend.)

9. We accept PayPal so you can use your credit card.

10. We are a Square Trade member committed to the highest levels of ethics, integrity, and customer service.

You'll also include one or more photographs of the item; more on that in the next chapter.

Formatting Your Listing

eBay will walk you through the mechanical process of creating your listing. Once you're comfortable with how to do it, you can use the tools we discussed in Chapter 6 to increase your speed and efficiency.

Your listing should be well-organized and easy to read—it doesn't have to be flashy or jazzy. Fancy borders, music, and graphics unrelated to your product are not necessary and may even be annoying to some shoppers. At the least, those elements make your listing open more slowly; at the worst, a shopper will quickly click out of a listing that is making noise if they're shopping at work or even at home late at night when the rest of the household is sleeping. Use colors, but do so carefully. You don't need a dizzying rainbow of text—you need clear information.

Write in bulleted lists rather than paragraph form. It's easier to read, and much easier for prospective customers to pick out the features that are important to them. Also, make your text right-justified instead of centered or full-justified and use a 12-point, easy-to-read font. If a prospective customer has to work too hard to figure out what you have to say, he'll probably move on to another item.

If you use an acronym in the headline (such as NIB), be sure to spell it out in the listing (new in box) in case your prospective bidder doesn't know what it means.

Once you have a style that works, use templates to make putting together your listings faster. For example, if you sell clothing, create a template that allows you to fill in all the standard information a buyer is going to want to know: size, color, manufacturer/designer, fabric content, where it was made, cleaning instructions, and measurements. For books, your template should allow you to quickly fill in the title, author, publisher, date published, and condition.

What to Leave Out of Your Listing

As important as thorough, complete listings are, there are some things you shouldn't include and some attitudes you should avoid.

Leave out photographs and text that you do not have the right to use. Using another seller's pictures or descriptions without permission is considered theft and is a violation of eBay's policies. In addition to auctions, this applies to store listings and About Me page content. So create your own pictures, and write your own copy.

Consider the impact on a prospective bidder of being rude or having mistakes in your listing. Take a look at the following text from an actual listing:

WE WANT OUR COSTUMERS TO BE AS REASONABLE AS WE ARE. IF YOU HAVE ANY PROBLEMS WITH OUR MERCHANDISE LET US KNOW BEFORE POSTING NEGATIVE FEED BACK, WE WILL TAKE EVERY EFFORT TO RESOLVE ANY ISSUES YOU MIGHT HAVE WITHIN WARRANTY PERIOD. FARTHER MORE WE RESPECT YOUR IMAGE AND POST EXCELLENT POSITIVE FEED BACK ON YOUR ACCOUNT. NEGATIVE FEED BACK POSTED TO UNREASONABLE COSTUMERS AND NONE PAYING BIDDERS. FOR COSTUMERS LEAVING NEGATIVE FEED BACK FOR FUN, WE RETURN A FAVOR WITH OUT FURTHER NOTICE AUTOMATICALLY, FURTHER MORE WE CONTACT EBAY AND SQUARE TRADE.

What's wrong with this message? Let's count the ways. First, typing in all caps is the equivalent of shouting in cyberspace—it's rude. Second, there is absolutely no excuse for misspellings such as "costumers" instead of "customers." Third, the threat about negative feedback is unnecessary and creates an ugly impression. If you walked into a retail store and the first thing the salesperson said to you was something similar to the above, would you feel welcome? Would you stay? Of course not.

Another seller includes the following auction terms in listings:

Failure to complete this transaction will result in negative feedback and "non-paying bidder" notification from eBay. Do NOT bid if you do not intend to purchase this item. Payment must be received within ten days of the Auction close. If payment is not received, you will automatically receive a non-paying bidder e-mail from eBay and your bid may be voided. All payments are carefully reviewed by our loss protection department. We reserve the right to deny shipment if necessary.

Before you even bid, you're being threatened with negative feedback and accused of making fraudulent payments—again, not a very friendly or welcoming approach.

Certainly if you run into a non-paying bidder, someone making a fraudulent payment, or any other illegal or unethical activity, you need to take the appropriate steps to deal with the situation. But these negatives don't need to be mentioned in your listing.

If You Make a Mistake in Your Listing

Mistakes happen—and especially when you're new to selling on eBay, you may find that you've launched an auction that includes either a mistake or the omission of some important information. Sometimes you'll discover this on your own; other times, it will be brought to your attention by potential bidders.

What you can revise depends on the time you have left before the listing ends, and whether or not the item has had bids or purchases.

If there are more than 12 hours before the auction listing ends, and you have received no bids or purchases, you can revise anything in your listing except the selling format. If your item has received a bid, a purchase, or ends within 12 hours, you can only add to the item description (you can't delete or change what is already there), add a second category, or add option seller features to increase the item's visibility.

Although you are not required to do this if you make a change, it would be courteous and good customer service to contact each bidder and let them know what you have added. Offer to cancel their bid if they are no longer interested due to the new information.

Another way to add or expand on information in your listing is when you are responding to e-mails from prospective buyers. When you are asked a question and you think other buyers may also be interested in the answer, you can display the question and answer publicly in your listing. Simply check the appropriate box when replying to the question before clicking on "submit." Your answer will be e-mailed directly to the person asking the question, and the five most recently added questions and responses will be displayed to the public on the item page.

Will You Sell Internationally?

Many eBay sellers restrict their sales to within their own countries, but you'll miss out on a lot of opportunities if you take this approach. An estimated one-third of eBay members are outside the United States, and many of them are willing to pay higher prices for items they can't get at home. The Walkers will sell to and ship anywhere in the world. "If somebody wants to buy something and have it sent to Mars and is willing to pay the shipping costs, we will certainly try to accommodate them," Ron Walker says. Gary Hunt (eBay User ID: speedwind) takes the same approach. "Thirty percent of our business goes overseas," he says. "If I didn't sell internationally, I wouldn't be anywhere near where I am today."

Challenges you might face by selling internationally include the additional work involved in packing and shipping, import/export rules, a longer transaction time, and language barriers. Even so, the additional work will usually pay off in higher sales. You must, however, do your homework and make sure your transaction doesn't violate any laws in the country of either the seller or buyer. Some items may require export licenses; others may be restricted as to the countries to which they can be shipped. Under U.S. law, there are a number of countries to which trade is either restricted or banned. But the United States has positive trade relations with most of the world—and that's good news for you as an eBay seller.

You can choose the countries where you will sell and indicate them when you post your listing. eBay will automatically post items to that country's eBay site—currently, eBay has sites in 24 countries. Keep in mind that "worldwide" means that you will sell anywhere. You can specify the currency in which you'll accept payment, although eBay lists your item in both currencies (yours and the other country's).

It's a good idea to create a "for international buyers" section in your listing with any special information an overseas customer may need to know. For more information about selling internationally, check out the International Trading Center on eBay or visit the U.S. Customs and Border Protection site at www.cbp.gov.

Choose Your Category

At any given moment, literally millions of items are up for sale on eBay in nearly 20,000 categories. Putting your auction in the correct category is essential if your particular listing is going to be viewed by the maximum number of potential buyers. Many bidders shop for specific items, but many others will browse categories, looking for things that just happen to catch their eye.

It may be appropriate to list a single item in more than one category. To find out what works best, browse around eBay and check the complete auctions of items similar to what you want to sell. Check the final sale price and the number of bids, and look for trends that would indicate that listing in one particular category gets better results than another.

Start by familiarizing yourself with eBay's top-level categories, and then get to know the subcategories that would be appropriate for your merchandise.

eBAY'S TOP-LEVEL CATEGORIES

Antiques	Health and Beauty
Art	Home and Garden
Books	Jewelry and Watches
Business and Industrial	Music
Cameras and Photo	Musical Instruments
Cell Phones	Pottery and Glass
Clothing, Shoes, and Accessories	Real Estate
Coins	Sporting Goods
Collectibles	Sports Memorabilia, Cards, and Fan Shop
Computers and Networking	Stamps
Consumer Electronics	Scripophily, U.S. and World Stamps
Crafts	Tickets
Dolls and Bears	Toys and Hobbies
DVDs and Movies	Travel
eBay Motors	Video Games
Entertainment Memorabilia	Everything Else
Gift Certificates	

Timing Is Everything

eBay may be a 24/7 marketplace, but your customers have shopping habits that you can identify and take advantage of when scheduling your auctions. Most bidding occurs in the last hour of an auction, so make sure that time period is when your customers are likely to be online. eBay traffic is typically high on weekends, so you may want to consider closing your auctions on Sunday evenings. Of course, if your customers are more likely to be shopping while at work during the day (either for themselves or for their companies), closing your auctions on weekday afternoons could be better.

Once you have your own track record to study, you can adjust your schedule based on what works best for you. If you are selling children's clothing, you may find that closing your auctions late on weekday evenings works well, because that's when busy mothers have the kids in bed and time to spend on the computer. Georgene Harkness (eBay User ID: mynewthreads) has found that the best ending times for her women's clothing auctions are Monday through Thursday, 10:00 A.M. to 4:00 P.M. "A lot of the women who buy from me are either at work behind a computer during the day, or at home when the kids are at school," she says. "I never have auctions end on the weekends, because I have found that I don't sell anything on the weekends."

When planning your closing time, keep time zones in mind. An 11:00 P.M. auction close for the California market is 2:00 A.M. for New Yorkers. You may miss out on a bidding war because the East Coast shoppers went to bed.

Another timing issue is how long your auctions run. Basic auctions can run for one, three, five, seven, or ten days. Fixed-price listings can run for three, five, seven, or ten days. Ideally, your auction should be up long enough to be seen by the maximum number of potential customers.

Some consumer items might do well with a three-day listing that starts Thursday evening and ends Sunday evening. For business products, a five-day listing that starts Sunday afternoon and closes Friday afternoon could be sufficient. Harkness uses seven-day listings to make sure her auctions get an entire week's exposure. "If I have a seven-day auction, everyone will have an opportunity to see it," she says. "But if I have a five-day auction that starts on Sunday night and ends on Friday night, then some people (weekend shoppers) will miss out."

Though seven-day auctions are the most popular, there are advantages to using the three-, five-, and ten-day listings, depending on your market and what you're selling. Auctions get the most exposure when they're first launched and just before they close. If you are selling common, popular merchandise, a three- or five-day listing may speed up your sales time. For collectible or unique items, especially those in the higher-value range, a ten-day auction gives bidders more time to find your item and research it or ask questions before bidding. While one-day auctions are available, you may miss potential buyers because of the time it takes for the listings to show up in searches.

Neubert believes three-day auctions are the best way to draw buyers into his eBay store. Those auctions are indexed and available by keyword and category search functions. By running them in a series on the core eBay site, he drives traffic to his store.

Experiment with different timing strategies to figure out what will work best for you.

It's Not Over When the Auction Closes

When the auction closes, you still have some work to do. Send an invoice to the winning bidder, collect your payment, get the item packaged and shipped, and then leave feedback for your buyer.

Second Chance Offer

If the winning bidder does not pay, if your reserve price was not met, or if you have duplicate items and you did not run a multiple-item auction, you may offer non-winning bidders a second chance at buying your item. In the case of a non-paying bidder, be sure you have done everything to resolve the situation before sending a second chance offer.

eBay does not charge a listing fee for second chance offers; you only pay the final value fee if the offer is accepted. Second chance offers contain a Buy It Now price equal to the non-winning bidder's bid amount.

If It Doesn't Sell

When an item doesn't sell—and not all of them will—you can relist it within 30 days of the closing date of the first listing. If it sells the second time around, you'll be credited for the insertion fee for the second listing. If it doesn't sell, you'll pay fees for both listings.

Don't just throw up the same listing that didn't work the first time. Consider lowering your starting bid, creating a different title, enhancing your description, or changing or adding photos.

CHAPTER 8

Take Photographs that Sell

A PICTURE IS WORTH A THOUSAND WORDS—corny, but true. And on eBay, a picture is worth serious dollars when it comes to what people are willing to pay for your merchandise. Certainly any picture is better than no picture— many eBay shoppers will not bid on an auction without a photo—but a quality picture will make a tremendous difference in the success of your auctions. In addition to letting bidders see what your product really looks like, quality photos also say that you're a serious, professional eBay seller.

"Pictures are more important than any description you put out there," Nona Van Deusen (eBay User ID: stylebug.com) says. eBay buyers can't see or touch the actual item you have for sale; they depend on the photograph to help them make bidding and buying decisions.

How important are quality photos? Van Deusen says she browses through eBay looking for gowns that are not photographed well, buys them, takes a good picture, and resells them for a profit.

Gallery Photos

eBay automatically adds the camera icon to listings with pictures so prospective bidders browsing through search results know when they click on your listing they'll be able to see what the product looks like. But many shoppers won't take that extra step—they want to see the product in the search results, and then decide if they want to click on the listing to learn more.

Using eBay's gallery feature allows you to add a thumbnail photo next to your listing so buyers can see your item without that extra click. eBay statistics show that gallery listings increase the final price by an average of 11 percent and are 9 percent more likely to sell—results that justify the nominal gallery fee for items that are likely to sell for more than a couple of dollars. Some eBay sellers use gallery photos for everything they auction; others use them for selected items, such as products they expect to sell for over a certain amount.

Set Up a Studio

If your goal is to become a high-volume eBay seller, your workspace should include a small photo studio for taking good pictures of your merchandise. It needs a neutral background screen and good lighting.

Cluttered backgrounds detract from your product and brand you as an amateur. Inexperienced eBay sellers may use a corner of their desk or the dining room table as a platform for their photographs, which means prospective buyers are likely to see the seller's personal items that have nothing to do with the product being sold.

Backdrops are easy and inexpensive to set up. For small items, a sheet of plain poster board will work. For larger items, try a bare wall, a solid-color bedsheet, or a painter's drop cloth. Or check out photography suppliers for professional backdrops.

At QuikDrop, a franchised eBay drop-off center, the photo station includes three backdrops: one solid light-colored, one solid dark-colored, and a green synthetic grass backdrop which is used for sporting goods and other items that may be used outdoors.

You may want to develop a photo background that helps brand your business. It could be a distinctive (but not distracting) color, it may have a subtle pattern, or it could include your logo or company name. Create a display pedestal for smaller items by draping a sturdy box with a piece of plain fabric.

Proper lighting is critical. Poor lighting prevents prospective bidders from seeing the detail they need to make a decision about whether and how much to bid. If a bidder isn't sure about what the item really looks like, he's likely to move on to an auction with a better picture. The best light is natural light. If necessary, add diffused artificial light, but never use a flash.

Van Deusen hired a professional photographer to consult with her on setting up her own in-house photography area. He made recommendations for backdrops, lighting, and other issues. After Van Deusen had purchased the recommended equipment, the photographer came back, helped her get it all set up, and showed her and her staff how to use everything appropriately.

Film or Digital?

If you don't have a digital camera when you're starting out, you can make do with a traditional film camera. You'll have to take your pictures, have them developed, then choose the images you want to use and scan them. Some photo processors will provide you with digital images from film for an extra charge. This is time-consuming and adds to your costs, so as soon as you can, invest in a good digital camera.

With a digital camera, you can instantly see your results—which means you won't have to restage your photos if they didn't turn out well. There are no film costs, and you can upload your images immediately.

You don't need a top-of-the-line digital camera, but you do need one that takes clear photos that adequately display your products. Get a brand name that you know and trust. Key features to look for include a resolution of 2.0 mega pixels or better, macro focus (the ability to take a clear picture from as close as one inch), and a manual flash (so you can take pictures without the flash). And, of course, shop for your digital camera on eBay.

Taking Your Photos

Take pictures from a variety of angles to show your item completely and accurately. In addition to the front view, consider pictures from the rear, sides, and top, as well as closeups of special details. Use a tripod to keep the camera steady and assure a sharp image.

Consider showcasing your item with accessories to display it to its best advantage. Put flowers in vases, books between bookends, and candles in candleholders. However, be sure the accessories do not distract from or hide any details of your products. Also, your listing should clearly indicate whether or not those accessories are included in the auction, available separately, or not for sale.

If the size of an item is not obvious, put something in the picture that will serve as a reference, such as a ruler or a coin. Invest in props that will enhance your photographs. For example, if you sell clothing or jewelry, consider buying used mannequins to properly display your items. You may even want to use live models, as Van Deusen does.

We started out with just headless mannequins, our lighting wasn't that great, and our pictures looked washed out," she recalls. "Then we switched to mannequins with heads and wigs, and we thought, 'Oh, this is wonderful.' But it still didn't seem quite right, because the clothes didn't fit them properly. Now we have live models, which is so much better. And we get so much more money for our garments when they're on a live model rather than a headless or regular mannequin with a face.

Editing Your Photos

Digital cameras and scanners come with graphics-editing software, or you can use free software, shareware, purchased software, or eBay's Picture Service to edit your pictures.

Crop (trim) your pictures to remove any unnecessary background and present a tight image of the item you have for sale. Rotate and resize as necessary until you have a clear, professional picture that shows off your merchandise to its best advantage.

Photo Don'ts

- Don't use the flash feature; it washes out details of the item being photographed. Instead, use strong ambient light that shows detail.
- Don't use photos from another eBay seller or from other web sites, including the item's manufacturer, unless you have permission from the owner of the image.

- Don't use stock photos, even if you have permission. Bidders prefer to see the actual item, not a scanned photo from a brochure.
- Don't get in the picture. If the item you're photographing is reflective (a mirror or glass or similar item), take the picture from an angle that assures the photographer is not in the final image.
- Don't edit your photographs in ways that would distort their accuracy.

Books and Other Flat Items

If you sell books and other flat items (such as collectible postcards, record albums, or photographs), you can scan the item with a flatbed scanner rather than taking a picture. Don't crop your scan too close, especially if the item shows wear along the edges. Be sure bidders can clearly see the item's condition.

Photo Hosting

You can store your photographs and manually insert them in each item listing, but a more effective and efficient approach is to use a photo-hosting service. Many of the auction management software programs and services include photo hosting as an option. Monitor the eBay discussion boards for tips on choosing a photo-hosting service.

eBay's Photo Services

eBay includes one photo in each auction listing and charges for additional images. Multiple pictures give you the opportunity to show your item from different angles. Depending on what you're selling, this may or may not be important—but statistics show that items with two or more pictures are 9 percent more likely to sell.

Adding pictures to your listings is quick and easy with eBay's Picture Services. You can also store and manage your photos with eBay Picture Manager, which is fully integrated with other eBay tools. Picture Manager is a subscription service with several plans based on storage size. The service also has a security feature that allows you to include a watermark on your photos of either the Picture Manager logo or your eBay User ID.

Other Photo-Hosting Services

You have plenty of independent photo-hosting services to choose from, many of which are less expensive than eBay's Photo Services, and a number of which are free. A free photo-hosting service that gets high marks from eBay users is www.photo bucket.com. Or, for an economical fee-based service designed for medium- to high-volume sellers with a large number of pictures, check out www.hostpci.com. Many auction management products also include image hosting. You might want to try several hosting services to decide which is best for you.

When choosing a photo-hosting service, find out if it has its own built-in program to upload pictures, or if you will need FTP (file transfer protocol) software to transfer images. Should you need FTP software, both WS_FTP (www.ipswitch.com) and FTP Voyager (www.ftpvoyager.com) are popular and easy to use.

Most major Internet Service Providers (ISPs) provide a limited amount of free web space to their members that can be easily used for uploading images. For small-volume sellers or someone just getting started on eBay, this is an excellent no-cost alternative for placing more than one picture in a listing.

If you have your own web site, use its storage space for hosting and storing images. Ron and Sheri Walker (eBay User ID: beansantiques) use their web site specifically for hosting their auction photos. "It's a very economical way to store all of our pictures," says Ron. Their site currently has approximately 9,000 images.

Make the Most of Each Picture

Once an auction has closed, don't discard the picture. You never know when that item will become available for sale again. Maintain a database of pictures so it's easy to pull up images for listings when you are selling items you've sold before. Van Deusen, for example, archives all her photographs. "We sort them by months, so if we get an item today that we got three months ago, we can go right to our archive and retrieve the picture."

~~~~~~

CHAPTER 9

Store It, Track It, Ship It

~~~~~~

A STRONG APPEAL OF SELLING ON EBAY and elsewhere online is the low cost and flexibility of operating in a virtual world. But if you sell merchandise, whether or not you have a brick-and-mortar retail operation, you need a place to store your merchandise; you also need to track your inventory, and you need a degree of shipping expertise so your products will arrive at their destination promptly and safely.

Storing Your Inventory

Unless you use a drop-shipper (see Chapter 5), you need space to securely store your products. How much space you need depends, of course, on what you're selling and the amount of inventory you keep on hand. It's also helpful if your storage area is roomy enough to function as a packing and shipping station. Your options include:

- *Space in your home.* If you are homebased and your merchandise doesn't take up a lot of room, you may have adequate storage space in your home. Designate a large closet or a room for your products. Many homebased eBay sellers work from their garages. For example, Karen Kelley (eBay User ID: thepinkboutique) has turned her garage into a small warehouse that accommodates thousands of pieces of merchandise. Seasonal items are kept in marked boxes until it's time to bring them out; garments ready to be auctioned hang on racks.

- *Self-storage facilities.* You can rent space equivalent to anything from a large closet to an extra garage at a self-storage facility. Many offer options ranging from air-conditioned space, indoor access, loading docks, and more. Some operators will accept deliveries on your behalf if you can't be there to sign for them yourself. Self-storage is a great option for a homebased business that needs a little extra space or even a retailer who wants storage at a lower price than at a commercial location. The self-storage industry is rapidly expanding and extremely competitive, so shop around before you make a decision.

- *Commercial warehouse space.* If you maintain a sizeable inventory and your items tend to be heavy, you may need a commercial warehouse facility with a shipping dock. You'll find this type of commercial space in industrial (light and heavy) parks and mixed-use commercial areas. Some offer only warehouse space; others have small offices and even showrooms adjacent to the warehouse. Gary Neubert (eBay User ID: gatorpack) has a 5,000-square-foot warehouse with a loading dock. After they closed their retail shop, Ron and Sheri Walker (eBay User ID: beansantiques) turned their building into what they call an "eBay factory" with a computer room, storage areas, and packing stations.

- *Public (commercial) storage.* A viable option to your own commercial space is a public warehouse. Public warehousing companies can essentially function as your shipping department. In addition to storage, their services include pick and pack operations, packaging, and labeling, and they will arrange for shipping on the carrier you specify. Public warehousing prices are based on usage—you only pay for the space and labor you use. Contract warehousing is similar in terms of services, but you pay fees whether or not you use space and services. Find public warehouse companies in your local telephone directory or through an internet search.

Remember that the more storage space you have, the easier it is to purchase off-season inventory that you hold until the time is right to sell. However, always remember to calculate storage costs into your cost of selling those items.

Whatever space you have designated for storage needs to be properly equipped and functional. You'll likely need sturdy shelves for boxes or bins, rods for hanging items, and a table to use for packing and labeling. Assign specific areas for items "to be listed," "listed," "sold, waiting for payment," and "ready to pack and ship."

Your storage facility's environment should be appropriate for your products. If your merchandise is temperature sensitive, make sure you use an air-conditioned facility. It should be dry, free of insects and other pests, and free of household odors such as cigarette smoke and pets.

Tracking Your Inventory

Do you know how Sam Walton became the world's most successful retailer? It wasn't because of a clever name, snazzy logo, creative ads, sharp frontline people, or even low prices—it was because of the company's superior inventory management. Business students in colleges and universities around the world study Wal-Mart's system, and smart companies copy it. Your own inventory management system doesn't have to be as high-tech or complex, but it does have to be as serious.

At any given moment, you need to know what you have on hand, what you've purchased that's on the way, what you need to buy, what's up for auction, what's available in your eBay store and on your web site, what's been sold, and what's been shipped.

For small, low-volume sellers, a simple index card system or spreadsheet will be sufficient. Serious eBay sellers track this information electronically. Most auction management software packages include inventory tracking.

In addition to keeping track of the information, you also need to consider the physical flow of your inventory. At QuikDrop, items move systematically through the store. After an item is accepted at the front counter, it goes to the photo area. Once it's photographed and the listing is written, it's moved to the area designated for items currently up for auction. When the auction closes, it's moved to the sold rack (or to the return-to-customer area if it didn't sell) until payment is received; then it goes to the shipping rack for packing and shipping.

Set up a system that works for the type of merchandise you're selling and that will allow you to be as efficient as possible.

Your inventory tracking system should tell you what's selling well—and what isn't. When items have overstayed their welcome in your warehouse, be creative about moving them out, even if you take a loss. For example, if Kathy Logan (eBay User ID: rosie_peachstate) has a craft supply product that isn't selling well, she will make something with it, and include a photo of that item in her auction listing to give potential buyers a better idea of what they can do with it. You can also put together groups of items and sell them in a single lot with a low starting bid, or offer a free bonus to the winning bidder. If you can't manage to sell it, donate it to charity—do whatever you have to do to free up your storage space and your cash for more products, even if it sometimes means taking a loss.

Nona Van Deusen (eBay User ID: stylebug.com) sells high-end designer clothes at deep discounts through a small retail store, a web site, and on eBay. "On eBay, we really drop the prices," she says. "We want to keep the merchandise moving out, keep it going. We don't want to hold on to it too long, because it's fashion—it comes in and out." She says you have to expect to take an occasional loss on a specific transaction. "We don't always sell things for a profit. We move things for a loss sometimes just to get rid of them."

"I don't necessarily believe that Circuit City profits on every sale that they do, or that Home Depot profits on every sale that they make," says Michael Jansma (eBay User ID: gemaffair). His point is that eBay sellers won't profit on every single sale, either. What's important is that your business earns an overall profit.

Getting It Out the Door

Once you've received payment for an item—and you never ship without being paid first!—it's time to pack and ship. Even though your customer usually pays the shipping costs, you need to handle this part of the transaction smoothly and efficiently.

Your inventory management system should include controls to make sure the correct merchandise is shipped to every customer. Neubert says sending items to the wrong place or not shipping the right product are costly mistakes. "We pride ourselves on the fact that we make very, very few errors by the way our operation is set up," he says. "And on the rare occasion a mistake is made, we view it as a customer service opportunity to emphasize how seriously we take our business."

However you handle it, ship promptly. The faster your buyer receives her item, the happier she will be. Georgene Harkness (eBay User ID: mynewthreads) says that she ships as soon as she receives payment. "If I get the money before noon on a particular day, their item will go out that afternoon," she says. "When people buy something, they want it now, so I try to do my part." Neubert also adheres to the "same day" shipping policy. "We guarantee that we will ship your order today as long as we receive your payment by 3:30 P.M. EST," he says.

Include shipping costs in your auction description or offer a shipping calculator so that bidders can determine how much it will cost to send a package to their zip code. If a potential buyer has to send you an e-mail to find how out much it will cost to ship something, they may just go to a listing that has the shipping amount clearly stated–especially if it is close to the end of the auction, which is when most bids are placed.

eBay has a free Shipping Calculator tool that can be added to your auction description. This includes rates for USPS and/or UPS and is based on the buyer's location. You can also include handling fees and insurance rates in the calculation.

Insurance

Many eBay sellers insist on insuring every package; others never buy insurance from the carrier but rather choose to self-insure. Some carriers (such as UPS and FedEx) include a minimal amount of insurance in their rates—typically $100—so you are insured for that amount without any additional cost or paperwork. Others (such as USPS and DHL) charge for insurance coverage from the first dollar.

Consider these issues when deciding whether to buy insurance:

- What is the risk of loss or damage to the merchandise you're shipping?
- What is the average value of your shipments?
- What is the average cost to insure your shipments (include both the cost of the coverage and the time it takes to do the necessary paperwork)?
- What would it cost you to replace an item if it were lost or damaged?
- How many shipments a week (or month) are you sending out?

Let's say you sell children's clothes, the average value of your shipments is $60, and you're shipping 100 packages a week by USPS. In a year, you'll spend more than $6,500 in insurance (at $1.30 per shipment). But your packages are not fragile; although it's possible to damage them, the real risk is loss. So if the Post Office loses one-half of 1 percent of everything you send, your cost to replace the merchandise is only $1,560—which means you're still ahead of the game by not buying insurance. And by not buying insurance, you keep your shipping costs lower than your competition.

Randy Smythe (eBay User ID: glacierbaydvd) charges a flat rate of $4.95 for shipments to the continental United States, regardless of how many DVDs are purchased. He doesn't buy insurance, he says, because DVDs are rarely damaged in transit and it's more efficient and profitable for him to absorb the loss than to buy insurance.

What about the possibility of a customer claiming the merchandise didn't arrive when it did? The fact is that most people are honest—and dealing with the few who aren't is just a cost of doing business.

Insurance is recommended for fragile or high-value merchandise. Some sellers allow their customers to make the decision of whether to insure; if you take this approach, make it clear that you will not be responsible for items that are lost or damaged in transit.

Delivery Confirmation

Delivery confirmation takes care of the question of whether a package was delivered. When purchased online, the cost is usually reduced and sometimes free. For higher-priced items, you may want to also require a signature on delivery.

Setting Your Shipping Fees

A common mistake among new eBay sellers is underestimating shipping and handling fees. When you don't charge enough for shipping, the difference comes out of your profit.

Many eBay sellers find it works best to charge a flat rate for shipping and choose the carrier themselves. They take a "time is money" approach and figure that if they occasionally lose a little money on shipping, they make up for it in time saved. Others offer options so their customers can decide how fast they want to receive their purchase and how much they are willing to pay for that speed. It's common for eBay sellers to offer what is called "combined shipping," which means they discount shipping costs if the buyer wins another auction or buys a second item from their eBay store.

A scale is essential for calculating accurate shipping costs. Get one large enough to accommodate at least the majority (if not all) of the items you sell. When Maggie Donapel (eBay User ID: plumsbooks) first started selling books on eBay, she would weigh them with what freight industry workers jokingly call "Toledo arms" (a reference to a well-known brand of scales)—that is, she would hold a book in her hand and guess how much it weighed. Unfortunately, her accuracy left much to be desired. After a few miscalculations, including one where what she lost in shipping was as much as her profit on the sale, she got a real scale. When weighing your items, be sure to include packing materials in your total weight.

In addition to the actual shipping, you may want to charge a handling fee, which is designed to cover your packaging costs (materials and time). As a seller, you'll need to buy supplies such as ink, labels, boxes, bubble wrap, foam peanuts, envelopes, tape, and more. You can either pay for these materials out of your profits or let your customers absorb the cost through a handling fee. If you decide to charge a handling fee, be sure to state "shipping and handling" in your auction terms—otherwise, a buyer may complain that what you're charging for shipping is higher than the actual cost.

Be reasonable when setting your shipping and handling fees. Resist the temptation to make this a profit opportunity. eBay may consider this an effort at fee avoidance, which is prohibited, and experienced buyers may recognize what you're doing and decline to bid on your auctions.

Kelley uses the free Priority Mail boxes provided by USPS, so she does not charge handling fees but rather for actual shipping costs only. "I do not gouge on shipping," she affirms. "I hate it when people do that to me, so I'm not going to do that to my customers."

Rather than charging the actual shipping cost, which can vary depending on where your customer is located, you may opt to calculate a midrange rate and set a flat fee for shipping with some amount for handling included. Harkness says, "I have found that my customers like it better if they have a flat fee and they don't have to figure out how much it is going to be."

Shipping Overseas

Many eBay sellers are reluctant to ship internationally because they are not familiar with the process. But limiting yourself to domestic sales means missing out on opportunities to bring in more bids and significantly increase your profits. International buyers may not be able to readily find the items you are auctioning and are often more than willing to increase their bids and pay high international shipping fees and handling charges. For most small-dollar-value items, the carrier you use to ship the item will assist you in completing the necessary paperwork.

International shipping rates vary dramatically, so don't try to flat-rate these charges. For example, a five-pound package sent airmail parcel post to Canada will cost $16.75 (plus insurance, pickup, and any appropriate document charges). That same package to Germany will cost $22.75; to India, $32.75; and to Botswana, $34.00. In the shipping section of your auction description, ask international bidders to contact you for a rate quote. International carriers, including USPS, UPS, FedEx, and DHL, have online rate calculators and additional information about exporting on their web sites. Sending merchandise to most overseas destinations is not difficult; it just requires the completion of a short declarations form.

It's important to be honest on your export documents. Some overseas buyers may ask you to mark an item as a gift or state a value that is lower than what you actually sold the merchandise for to reduce the amount of import duty they have to pay. Don't do this—it's illegal.

Choosing a Carrier

One of the world's largest industries is transportation, so it's obvious that you'll have a mind-boggling array of choices when it comes to shipping your goods. Before you make a decision on which carrier to use, take the time to become familiar with the pricing and service levels of various package and freight carriers. Remember that your choice of carrier is a reflection of your overall operation, so use one that delivers a high level of customer service and reliability. Don't make your decision on cost alone—the lowest price is not always the best value.

It's important to understand the difference between a package carrier and a common carrier. Package carriers (such as UPS, FedEx, and USPS) handle smaller shipments with per-package weight limits typically ranging from 70 to 150 pounds. Most offer a choice of ground or air service. Common carriers are truck lines that handle large, heavy shipments too big for the package carriers.

When making your carrier selection, consider these points:

- What are the size and weight limitations, and how do they compare with what you are shipping?
- What levels of service are available, and do they meet your needs?
- Does the carrier offer volume discounts or other incentives?
- Does the carrier offer online shipment tracking? Most do, so also consider how easy or difficult it is to use. Also, does the carrier offer e-mail notification to let your customer know the shipment is en route?
- Will the carrier make multiple delivery attempts without charging extra?
- Does the carrier deliver on Saturdays, and if so, is there an extra charge?
- Does the carrier deliver to residences, and if so, is there an extra charge?
- For heavier items, will the carrier bring the shipment inside? Typically, package carriers leave items at the door; common carriers may not deliver beyond the truck's tailgate, and if they do, they may charge.
- How late will the carrier make pickups at your facility, and how does this blend with your work schedule?
- Does the carrier have a facility where your customers can pick up their packages?
- Does the carrier offer return services to help you retrieve packages if necessary?
- Will the carrier provide delivery confirmation, and if so, is there an extra charge?
- Is the carrier financially stable with well-maintained equipment and qualified staff?

As important as carrier selection is for what you are shipping out, it is equally important for what you receive. If you are paying the freight on your incoming supplies and merchandise, you have the right to choose the carrier.

Opening an Account

Set up an account with the carrier(s) you'll be using. This not only makes the shipping process easier, but it is also a way for you to negotiate volume discounts. The easiest way to set up an account is on the carrier's web site, but that's not always the smartest way. Insist that the carrier send a sales representative to meet with you in person to discuss your needs—and let the salesperson know you are also meeting with other carriers. Depending on your volume, you may qualify for discounts as high as 40 percent, as well as other services, including the use of a label printer, packaging materials, and daily pickups.

Packing

Good packing is essential to protect your merchandise while it's in transit. Using adequate, quality materials and careful packing tells your customers that you believe their purchase is of value—regardless of whether they bought a 99-cent trinket or a $2,000 piece of equipment. It also increases the chances that your items will arrive in good condition—which eliminates the hassle of complaints and damage claims.

As you pack, remember that your packages are going to be on a truck with other packages. They'll probably be loaded and unloaded several times, they'll likely experience bumps and vibrations, they may have other boxes stacked on top of them, and they may get dropped or tossed around repeatedly. "Fragile" stickers and "This end up" marks will not protect a carelessly packed shipment from damage.

Use sturdy, corrugated boxes and cartons that can be completely sealed with packing tape. Pack individually wrapped items in layers, with the heaviest on the bottom and the lightest on top. There should be enough space between the item and the wall of the box for padding, such as paper, packing peanuts, or bubble wrap to absorb shocks.

Fragile items need extra TLC, including double-boxing. Buyers usually will not mind paying the additional handling fees that come with this type of special attention. Don't pack bulky or heavy items together with fragile ones. Newsprint paper is a quick and easy way to wrap items and provides an additional layer of protection when combined with bubble wrap. You can use regular newspaper, but there is always the danger of ink rubbing off on the product. Plain newsprint can be purchased from packing supply houses, or may be available from your local newspaper.

When preparing your packages for shipping, include the addresses of both the sender and the recipient on shipping labels. You may also want to put an extra label on the inside of the box in the event something happens to the outside label and it can't be read. Also, if there is more than one box, number them accordingly (example: Box 1 of 3, Box 2 of 3, Box 3 of 3).

Labeling

Thanks to new and constantly improving online shipping tools, most sellers can print labels from their computers rather than creating them by hand. Adhesive labels are sturdier than printing on plain paper and taping that to the box. A newer option is "weatherproof" labels, but they have been getting mixed reviews. Many users complain that it takes too long for the ink to dry and that smudging is almost inevitable.

Stamps.com (www.stamps.com) and Endicia Online Postage (www.endicia.com) are two of several timesaving postage systems for sellers who ship a high volume of items. You can print out labels with any type of official USPS postage (i.e., Express, Media, First Class) to be delivered anywhere in the world. They offer competitive monthly subscription fees and free trial periods.

USPS (www.usps.gov) has a "Click-N-Ship" feature that will print out labels with postage and insurance for Priority, Express, or Global (international) Mail by using your credit card. You can also download a free software program called "Shipping Assistant" that can be used to calculate domestic and international rates using any of the postal services, including First Class, Media Mail, and Parcel Post, as well as Priority and Express Mail. Most major couriers such as United Parcel Service (www.ups.com) and FedEx (www.fedex.com) have similar online features, plus you can often schedule pickups from your home or office online without having to make a phone call.

There are many other auction management tools that will also calculate postage and print out labels with or without postage. PayPal and eBay have a combined feature at the close of the auction where you can go to the auction page or My eBay and simply click a link to generate a label. This will print out a shipping label with the buyer's name and address and precalculated postage on it without having to type anything other than your password. There is a nominal processing fee that will be deducted from your PayPal account along with the postage, but the time savings may be worth it.

Liz Baker (eBay User ID: theliteratelady) prefers using the USPS Shipping Assistant calculator to predetermine shipping costs because it's quick and easy. "But when it's time to mail out a package, I let PayPal handle all those little details for me with just a couple of clicks," she says.

Supplies

When you're starting out, you may want to look for inexpensive and free sources of shipping supplies. Although experts advise using only new boxes, many eBay sellers reuse boxes with great success. Just make sure that the box is in good condition, remove old labels, and completely scratch out or eliminate any other identifying markings. You may even want to completely dismantle the box, turn it inside out, and tape it back together for a "fresh" look. Or you can purchase maskout paint that can be sprayed on boxes to cover up old markings and make them look like new.

Shred your used giftwrap, junk mail, and other paper and use it as filler in your packages. Let friends and family members know you can use packing materials—they may be able to collect used sturdy boxes and packing peanuts from where they work. Visit furniture stores and ask if you can have their used bubble wrap. Most will be glad to give it to you because it would otherwise get tossed in the trash bin.

Most package carriers have a selection of boxes and other supplies available at no charge for certain service levels. The USPS, for example, provides free boxes for Express and Priority Mail shipments; however, it is against the law to use those boxes for any other purpose. Ask carriers what they provide and what restrictions apply.

Logan never purchases packing materials because she has always been able to find used boxes and bubble wrap at various stores and businesses. And she likes being able to pass this cost savings on to her customers. "I always use USPS First Class Mail because it's cheaper than Priority Mail," she says. "And since I don't have to purchase packing supplies, I only charge a very small handling fee."

However, the Walkers say that with the volume of shipping in their business, they simply do not have time to go out and hunt for boxes, so they buy their materials in bulk from a local vendor. As your own volume grows, you'll need to purchase your packing supplies from a specialty vendor.

CHAPTER 10

Customer Service the eBay Way

eBAY BUYERS DEMAND—and enjoy—a high level of customer service, and if you're going to succeed in selling on eBay, you need to take care of your customers. On eBay, your customer satisfaction rating is posted on your front door through the feedback system. This allows buyers and sellers to leave comments about each other that are visible to all other eBay users.

Think about it. When you walk into a retail store, whether it's a small independent operation or a national chain, you have absolutely no idea what percentage of customers are happy and what percentage are not. But when you look at a product on eBay, you know immediately how happy that seller's customers are—and the unhappy customers are usually very specific about what went wrong with the transaction.

In fact, many large traditional retailers have not done well on eBay because they are happy if just 90 percent—or even fewer—of their customers are satisfied.

But a feedback rating of anything below the high 90s is the kiss of death for an eBay seller.

Make customer service your number-one priority, and expect it to take more time than you think. For every auction you put up, you're probably going to get at least two e-mails that have to be answered personally—and promptly. If you see a pattern in the questions, address those issues in your product descriptions, on your About Me page, or in your eBay store. You can also develop standard responses you can cut and paste into e-mails to speed up the response time for your answers.

Jonathan Garriss (eBay User ID: gothamcityonline) says customer service on eBay is "much more intensive" than when you're selling through other channels. eBay shoppers tend to ask more questions and require more hand-holding. If a question doesn't get answered before your auction closes, the customer probably won't bid. And because procedures for completing a transaction (payment method, shipping issues, etc.) vary significantly among eBay sellers, Garriss says, "You have

FIGURE 10.1: **AFTER-THE-SALE CHECKLIST**

❏ Send an invoice.

❏ Make second-chance offers if you have extra products.

❏ Receive payment.

❏ Package item with appropriate inserts.

❏ Ship as promised.

❏ Notify buyer that item has been shipped.

❏ Leave feedback.

❏ Do follow-up marketing to turn first-time buyers into repeat customers.

to work very hard to convey your message of what to do next and how to complete the order." See Figure 10.1

The smartest thing Georgene Harkness (eBay User ID: mynewthreads) ever did was to make customer service the most important part of her eBay business. She read two books by Stanley Marcus, *Quest for the Best* and *Minding the Store* (University of North Texas Press), and decided to follow his advice about offering the best in goods and services—and it's paid off in profits. "I'm not selling anything on the scale of Neiman-Marcus, but the principles behind Marcus' theories hold true for everyone," she says. "If a person wants to be a successful seller, she is going to have to pay attention to the buyer."

Though your first impression typically comes with your auction listing, your last—and final—impression is made when the product is delivered. Steve Mack (eBay User ID: ztradingpost) says his stores package used items as though they were new, shrink-wrapping and boxing in a way that will protect the merchandise and impress the buyer. Your product may be exactly—or even better—as you described, but if it arrives wrapped in used paper, packed in an old kitty litter box, your customers may think twice about buying from you again.

Customer Service Basics

Whether your business consists exclusively of auctions or you also sell from an eBay store, your own web site, or even a brick-and-mortar store, the basic principles of customer service remain the same:

- *See your business through your customers' eyes.* Is your operation user-friendly, efficient, and responsive? Garriss says that with their questions and high expectations, eBay customers will force you to thoroughly understand your business processes.
- *Ask what your customers want and need.* Don't assume that you know what your customers want. Ask them—and listen to their answers.
- *Meet or exceed expectations.* When you promise to do something—whether it's provide information, ship a product, or something else—do as you promised, or better.
- *Ask if there's anything else you can do.* When the transaction is complete, find out if you can provide any other product or service. A simple "Is there

anything else I can help you with?" via e-mail or on a note enclosed in the package can net you additional sales and invaluable goodwill.

- *Keep in touch.* Let your customers know that they are important to you after the sale is complete and you've gotten their money. Many successful eBay sellers send newsletters letting customers know when new products are available.
- *Be a copycat.* Pay attention to good customer service when you receive it, whether it's in a restaurant, the grocery store, or elsewhere, and duplicate those techniques in your own operation.

What's Special about eBay Customer Service?

The big difference between customer service on eBay and when you sell through other channels is that most of your communications with eBay users are handled via e-mail. That means your written communication skills must be excellent—even though you'll often be dealing with people who aren't quite as clear and who may not always make sense.

The need to promptly answer inquiries about your auctions or store listings cannot be emphasized too strongly. People who have a question about your product may not bid until it's answered. You need to answer questions quickly so potential customers still have time to place a bid.

The default order of eBay search results lists items by those ending soonest. So you may have a shopper who finds your auction with just hours to go and has a question. Liz Baker (eBay User ID: theliteratelady) says this happens to her often when she's shopping on eBay. "I'll do a search and something will come up that I'm interested in but I want more information and the auction ends in just a few hours," she says. "I'll send an e-mail, but I don't always get an answer. When the seller doesn't answer, I don't bid. But if my question had been answered, I might have been willing to pay more than the winning bidder. In fact, I've started a few last-minute bidding wars because I found something I wanted and the seller answered my questions quickly."

A growing challenge for eBay sellers is the increasing popularity of spam filters—which may filter out a seller's response to a buyer's question. You may want to include a statement in your listings to address this, such as, "We are happy to respond to questions by e-mail. If you ask a question, be sure your spam filter is set to allow mail from unknown addresses. If you do not hear from us within four hours (during normal business hours), please resend your question and check your spam filter."

Though prompt response to e-mails is a critical element of good customer service on eBay, if you have a full-time job, you may not be able to answer e-mails related to your eBay business while you're at work. Let your potential customers know your situation and when to expect to hear from you. You can include a statement in your listings, on your About Me page, or as part of your signature line in e-mails. It can say something like, "Your total satisfaction is my goal. In addition to my eBay business, I have a full-time job and therefore am able to answer e-mails only from 6:00 to 11:00 P.M. Eastern time, Monday through Friday, and from 8:00 A.M. to 7:00 P.M. on Saturday. Your questions and requests are important to me, and I will respond to you as soon as possible. Thank you for your patience and understanding."

If your product is one that is typically purchased during an emotional or stressful time, be prepared to deal with emotional and stressed-out customers. For example, brides shopping for wedding gowns and accessories or pregnant women shopping for nursery furnishings may be anxious about their purchases—and that anxiety may translate into rudeness and excessive demands. Don't take it personally. Answer the questions, and if there's a problem, fix it.

When you start to see a pattern in the questions you receive by e-mail, go back to your listings and see if you can address those issues either there or on your About Me page. If you are consistently leaving out similar information even on different products, redesign your template so you'll remember to include it. You may also develop standard responses in your word processing program that can easily be pasted into an e-mail and quickly customized for the particular situation.

Of course, the best listings in the world won't stop e-mails from people who didn't bother to read all the details. Be prepared for questions that are clearly answered in your listing—such as, "How many carats of diamonds are in those half-carat diamond earrings?" and "Is this product new or used?" (when your listing specifically says "new"). Keep your sense of humor, and resist the urge to write something like, "If you had read the listing, you would already know that."

Kathy Logan (eBay User ID: rosie_peachstate) once had a customer ask, "What are your bamboo beads made of?" While this seems like a no-brainer on the surface, it's possible the customer was really asking if the bamboo beads were authentic or a plastic imitation. Whatever the motivation, Logan did the smart thing: she simply answered the question—the beads were indeed made of bamboo—and then added a few more details that were also in the description, in case the customer missed them. Logan's friendly message gave the customer the information she wanted and enabled her to bid with confidence.

Set up an automated system to let your customers know what is going on with their purchases. E-mail them when you receive their payment, to tell them when you're going to ship, then send them a tracking number when you have shipped. "Make the buyer feel like they're involved in the whole process," advises Nona Van Deusen (eBay User ID: stylebug.com). This is especially important for first-time customers who don't yet know for sure that you are trustworthy.

"Our service has to be ten times better than a brick-and-mortar store," says Michael Jansma (eBay User ID: gemaffair). "There are two reasons for that. One is that customers are not walking into our store. There is no chance to get a feel of our tile, the nice lights, the attractive staff standing behind the counter, our $10,000 worth of showcases, the flowers, the music on the radio, the plaza the store is in—we don't have any of that. We only have our feedback and some text. That's it. The second thing we have to overcome is [the desire for] instant gratification. Nobody can walk in, try on some earrings, and wear them to a class reunion that night. A guy can't buy an engagement ring [on eBay] and propose with it that night. Your feedback, your communication with that customer, and the way you present your ad is everything on eBay."

Treat all your communications with other eBay users as business correspondence, and remember that the structure, tone, and details of your e-mails are a reflection of your operation. Begin your messages with a salutation, write in complete sentences, don't use slang or abbreviations your customer may not understand, end with a proper closing, and proofread and spell-check—then proofread again before you hit "send."

Dealing with Difficult Customers

Is the customer always right? Of course not—but he's always the customer. When you have a customer who is being difficult and demanding, work with him as best you can, but don't allow yourself to be browbeaten or threatened into violating your own policies.

When you sell on eBay, you will often deal with people who are not accustomed to shopping on the internet or who may be new to eBay. A customer may be difficult due to his or her basic nature, but another may give you a hard time because she doesn't know any better and is apprehensive about the transaction. Being proactive with your communications will go a long way toward heading off complaints that are based on fear.

There will be times when you have a bad customer and you just have to deal with it. It happens to every retailer in every venue at one time or another. You may just have to bite the proverbial bullet and say, "I've done everything I said I would do, I've tried my best to make you happy, but it's clear that I cannot please you." Then make your final offer to resolve the situation (perhaps a refund or an exchange), give the customer a deadline to accept, and let it go. If the customer leaves you negative feedback, you can post a response to it. You can also check to see if that particular eBay user chronically leaves negative feedback for sellers, and point that out in your response.

Difficult customers are just part of being in business—whether you operate on eBay or anywhere else. Don't let them get to you. And when you are struggling with a complaining and unreasonable customer, stop for a minute and read all the positive feedback your other customers have left. That will help you put things into perspective and give you the boost you need to keep going.

That Special Difficult Customer: The Non-Paying Bidder

Most eBay buyers understand that a bid is an obligation to purchase, and most will pay with reasonable promptness after the auction closes. After all, they're excited about what they've bought and eager to receive their merchandise. eBay and PayPal have made the payment process simple and easy, so most customers will pay when they receive the winning bid notification. But there are those rare bidders who, for a variety of reasons, take their time paying—or don't pay at all.

When a payment isn't made promptly, give your customers the benefit of the doubt—at least in the beginning. Your payment terms in your auction listing should clearly state the deadline for payment, and you should repeat that information in your winning bid notice/invoice. Most sellers require payment within three to ten days of the close of the auction. Giving your customers a reasonable time to make a payment gives them a chance to add to their purchase through other auctions or your eBay store.

If you have not received payment by the due date, send a follow-up notice. You can create your own notice, or use the standard payment reminder eBay provides, but be nice about it. There are a wide range of reasons for a buyer to not pay right away—a sudden illness, a personal crisis, or even a computer crash are all legitimate and understandable reasons for a delayed payment. During the hurricane season of 2004 in Florida, many buyers were unable to make payments when the storms knocked out electricity for days unexpectedly. A nasty note from you can make an unfortunate situation even worse. A gentle reminder will usually get the payment made, and if it doesn't, you need to implement your non-paying bidder procedure. For example, your policy may be that anything not paid for within ten days is returned to inventory and relisted for sale.

You will occasionally encounter bidders who are unable to pay or who change their minds after winning an auction and decide to default. It may be that the bidder caught "auction fever" and bid more than he could afford. Or a bidder decides that she doesn't really want the item or can get a better deal on it elsewhere.

When a bidder doesn't pay in the amount of time you stipulate in your terms and does not respond to payment reminders, you are free to relist the item and sell it to someone else. You can also make a second chance offer to the second place bidder, if you're willing to accept that amount. In either case, be sure to file a non-paying bidder alert with eBay and leave appropriate feedback for the buyer. Non-paying bidder alerts may be filed at least seven days but nor more than 45 days after the auction closes. When you file a non-paying bidder alert, you may also request a credit for the final value fee for that transaction. You should also place a non-paying bidder on your blocked bidder list, so you don't have to deal with that person in the future.

Protection Programs

There are a number of programs to make buying and selling on eBay safe and worry-free. If you have a problem with a transaction, go to eBay's Security and Resolution Center for assistance and direction.

You may also want to register with Square Trade, eBay's dispute resolution service. For a small monthly fee, you are entitled to include the Square Trade seal in your listings, which tells potential buyers your identity has been verified, you are committed to meeting high standards and resolving issues quickly before turning to negative feedback, and you will use mediation if the need arises. As a Square Trade member, Karen Kelley (eBay User ID: the pinkboutique) believes displaying the seal is reassuring to buyers. "People see that logo and they know I am committed to working out any problems," she says.

Your Policies Are Part of Your Service

The policies you establish are the foundation of your customer service. Your policies should be fair, reasonable, and clearly stated. As an eBay seller, your two most important policies when it comes to customer service are your shipping policy (discussed in Chapter 9) and your return and refund policy.

Creating a Return and Refund Policy

The easiest—but not necessarily the best—return and refund policy is: "All Sales Final." The fact is, such a statement will make most buyers think twice about doing business with you. After all, buyers are purchasing something they can't see or touch from someone they don't know, and you're saying, "Hey, if you're not happy, too bad."

A better approach is a return and refund policy that is fair to both your customer and you. Put an abbreviated version of your return and refund policy in every listing, and a full explanation on your About Me page.

For example, in your listing, you could say, "We guarantee all of our merchandise and will gladly take back any item with which you are not completely satisfied. For complete information on our Return and Refund Policy, see our About Me page."

Your full return and refund policy should include a time limit (such as, "we accept returns within 30 days of receipt"), a description of the circumstances under which items can be returned, who pays for the original shipping and the return shipping costs, whether you charge a restocking fee, and any procedures customers must follow to return an item. Important: If your return policy promises refunds to dissatisfied customers, you are required by law to issue those refunds when they are requested.

For inexpensive items or merchandise you don't want back, consider negotiating a partial refund if an unhappy customer agrees to keep the product. Also, remember the long-term value of a customer when making a decision on refunds and returns. If a customer wants to return something—maybe a garment didn't fit

FIGURE 10.2: SAMPLE RETURN AND REFUND POLICY

Use this sample return and refund policy as a basis for creating your own. Be sure to insert your contact information and other specifics where appropriate.

Customer satisfaction is our number-one goal, which is why we provide a 30-day, no-questions-asked, money-back guarantee on our products. If for any reason you are not satisfied with your purchase, notify us by e-mail or phone, and we will promptly issue a Return Merchandise Authorization (RMA). The RMA is required for us to accept your return. Any item listed as "all sales final" will not be accepted for return, and no refund or credit will be issued. Returned seasonal or sale items will be eligible for store credit only. Under some circumstances, a restocking fee may be charged. Shipping charges are not refundable unless the return is due to our error.

Refunds are made in the same form as your payment and will be issued within seven days of our receipt of the returned merchandise. If your payment was made by personal check, your refund will be held until we can confirm your check has cleared. You may always choose a store credit instead of a refund.

To assist us in expediting your return, exchange, and/or refund, we ask that you

- contact us prior to returning the merchandise for an RMA number.
- return the merchandise to us within 30 days of the date you received it.
- return products in their original packaging in resalable condition.
- include all accessories, instructions, and other related items with your return.
- include a copy of the invoice and/or packing slip.
- mark the RMA number clearly on the outside of the box so we can easily identify your package when it arrives and handle your return promptly.

or a piece of equipment didn't work properly—and you make it difficult, you've probably lost a customer. But if you're cooperative and helpful, that customer will likely buy from you again.

Typically, original shipping is not refunded, and the customer pays for return shipping. However, if the item is defective or misrepresented, then shipping costs should also be refunded. You may also want to consider offering merchandise credits instead of cash refunds. See Figure 10.2.

Feedback

One of the key differences between selling on eBay and on any other venue is eBay's feedback system that lets every prospective customer know what all your other customers think about you. Smart buyers will always check your feedback rating before placing a bid. As a seller, especially if you're dealing with high-value items, you may want to check your bidders' feedback ratings before your auction closes. If a bidder has a substantial amount of negative feedback from other sellers, you may consider canceling the bid and putting the user on your blocked bidder list.

Some sellers will not accept bids from users with no or limited feedback. In addition to being unfair, this could cost you sales. Jim Salvas (eBay User ID: camerajim) says, "Everyone was new at one time, and it's hard to predict who is going to be a problem bidder."

A better alternative would be to write to a "newbie" who places a bid, wish her luck on your auction and gently remind her of your terms and conditions. Ask her to respond within 24 hours with any questions she may have and to indicate she understands your terms. If you don't hear back from her in a reasonable time before the end of your auction, you have time to make a judgment call on whether you want to cancel the bid and add this user to your blocked bidders list.

You have the opportunity to leave feedback on any completed transaction, as either the buyer or the seller. Of course, you are not required to do so—but this system is one of the key elements that makes eBay the special business venue it is.

How often have you gone into a brick-and-mortar store and asked for references? Chances are you have no idea what the customer satisfaction ratio is of most of the stores where you shop. But if there was a sign on the door of a store that said more than 98 percent or maybe only 75 percent of their customers were happy—would that affect your decision to do business there? Probably. When a number of large retailers first tried selling on eBay, they did not do well because they weren't used to having a customer satisfaction ratio posted on the front door. Most quickly figured out that they had to maintain a high feedback score; those that didn't aren't selling on eBay anymore.

"Every one of my customers gets the chance to look at what every one of my other customers has ever thought about me," Jansma says. "That just doesn't happen in the real world." There will always be customers who threaten to leave negative feedback if you don't do what they want—even when they're wrong or unreasonable. Some eBay sellers cave in to these requests; others don't. It's a judgment call only you can make. Keep in mind that your feedback rating is based on percentages, so the more positive feedbacks you have, the easier it will be for you to sustain one or two negative comments.

Honesty is critical to the integrity of the feedback system. Some sellers have been known to create fake User IDs so they can buy from themselves and place glowing testimonials about themselves in the feedback section of eBay and in the comment section of other auction sites. This is both unethical and fraudulent—don't do it.

Although many eBay sellers leave feedback as soon as they receive payment and ship the product, a growing number will not post feedback until the transaction is complete and the buyer has posted feedback about the seller. The thought among sellers is that this protects them against the possibility of negative feedback and gives them a chance to respond in kind if indeed the buyer does post a negative comment. At what point you leave feedback is your decision—and the best way to protect yourself against negative feedback is to provide excellent products and great service.

eBay's Feedback Policies

eBay is not legally responsible for the content of feedback postings and will only consider removing feedback if it violates the site's policies. When leaving feedback, you may not

- use inappropriate language, including profanity, patently vulgar language, or language that is racist, hateful, sexual, or obscene.

- make references to an eBay or law enforcement investigation. For example, you can't write, "The FBI is investigating this person" in your feedback remarks.
- publish contact information.
- include pictures, JavaScript, or links of any kind.

It is also against eBay's policy to bid on or purchase an item for the sole purpose of gaining the opportunity to leave negative feedback for the seller when the buyer has no intention of completing the transaction. Although eBay does allow you to respond to feedback and it's a good idea to do so when you receive a negative post, you may not post responses on other transactions to make additional remarks about a different transaction.

The Value of Subsequent Sales

In an ideal world, every sale would be equally—and highly—profitable. But we don't live in an ideal world. In most cases, repeat business is going to be more profitable than the initial sale because there are costs involved in capturing a new customer that are not duplicated when that customer makes another purchase. You need systems in place to encourage repeat business.

At least a third of Logan's customers are repeat buyers. "I've never had any problems with people that I could not work out," she says. "I run my business like a mom-and-pop store, and some of my buyers are now friends who will send me an e-mail and ask what I'm doing over the weekend." That kind of loyalty is priceless—and very profitable.

Make it easy for your customers to shop with you. Accept the payment methods they prefer, make your listings easy to read and your photographs clear, and establish a return policy that makes customers feel safe. Quality merchandise, careful packing, and prompt shipping will bring customers back. You might also offer discounts on future purchases or referral credits to encourage repeat business.

CHAPTER 11

Tell the World: Marketing Your eBay Business

"IF A MAN CAN WRITE A BETTER BOOK, preach a better sermon, or make a better mousetrap than his neighbor, though he builds his house in the woods, the world will make a beaten path to his door." These words, attributed to Ralph Waldo Emerson, are widely quoted to stress the importance of having a great product or idea for your business. But the reality is that if the world doesn't know you've built that proverbial better mousetrap, no one is going to be slogging through the woods to find you. To attract customers to your eBay business, you have to market. And the process of marketing your eBay operation can be as creative and as much fun as putting up items for sale.

Who Are You? Your "About Me" Page
One of eBay's best and most underutilized marketing tools is the About Me page. There is no charge to create an About Me page; all you have to do is register as a

seller. Use this page to tell potential customers about yourself, your expertise, your company, what other auctions you have, or how to get to your web site or store. You can also provide complete details on your policies, terms, and conditions that would be too cumbersome to include in each individual listing. This is an online brochure that lets your potential customers get to know you and feel comfortable dealing with you. Because no one can physically walk into your eBay identity, your About Me page is the next best thing to a personal introduction.

Ron Walker (eBay User ID: beansantiques) says that people like to know they are dealing with professionals, so he and his wife try to convey that image on their About Me page. "Since we do a lot of estate sales, we will include recent pictures of those on this page," he says. "We also let them see pictures of our eBay world, which include our packing rooms, photo rooms, and computer room. I think this lets visitors know we are serious about what we're doing." Walker also includes a number of strategically placed links on his About Me page that will take browsers to everything he is currently selling on eBay.

You can also use your About Me page to build a subscriber base by inviting visitors to sign up for your free newsletter (more on that later) or tell about an online discussion forum that may be of interest. The page also includes a short list of your current auctions and most recent feedback; the visitor does not have to click on any additional links to see that information.

In your auction description, encourage shoppers to visit your About Me page by offering information or special incentives. You might, for example, offer a small discount on shipping or some other bonus if the winning bidder can give you a special code found on your About Me page.

If you are an eBay affiliate, your About Me page can include dynamic links to some of your favorite auctions. Don't worry about sending customers to your competitors; using this strategy means that you will actually make a commission on any sales. Of course, always be sure that any links are in compliance with eBay policies. For example, you cannot place links to other third-party affiliate programs on any eBay page, including your auction listings, store, or About Me pages, nor can you promote non-eBay merchandise. However, you may direct visitors to your own personal web site that has links to products offered outside of eBay. You can also provide affiliate links to other eBay subsidiaries such as Elance.com, Half.com, and PayPal.com.

You can design your own About Me page or use one of the templates eBay provides. If you are not familiar with HTML, the templates will let you quickly and easily create an attractive page. However, the most effective About Me pages are set up to look like a separate web page that has the added bonus of featuring the eBay logo and menu bar.

When you have created your About Me page, a "me" icon will appear next to your User ID whenever it is shown on an eBay page. A click on that icon lets anyone read all about you and your business. You can also feature the About Me URL (http://members.ebay.com/aboutme/userID) in your auction descriptions, on web sites, in signature lines, on discussion boards, or anywhere else you want to be visible as an eBay seller.

About Me pages can be changed and updated at any time, no matter what type of auction activity is taking place. Be sure the information on your About Me page is always current and consistent with what you have in your auctions and your store.

Your Own Web Site

If you're serious about your online business, you need an online presence in the form of your own web site. In most cases, not having a web site limits your exposure and growth potential. In addition to credibility, a web site gives you a variety of marketing opportunities.

Strategically placed links on your web site will attract non-eBay customers to your auctions and eBay store. Direct eBay users who have checked out one of your auctions, your store, or your About Me page to your web site to see what other products and services you offer that may be of interest. You can also take advantage of eBay's affiliate program (see Chapter 13) by placing links on your site to other auctions that complement your site. As you develop your site, consider these points to make it one of your most powerful marketing tools.

Paid Host versus Free Host

Free is good, right? Not when it comes to web site hosting. A "free" host is never actually free. The host has to make money somehow, and the most common way is with those annoying, flashy banners and pop-up sponsor ads that have absolutely nothing to do with your business, but will be the first thing visitors to your site will see. You have absolutely no control over the ad content, and some of it can be quite inappropriate. You'll also find that most free hosts offer very little, if anything, in the way of technical support.

Free sites are typically very limited in the amount of space you have. Most allow no more than three pages and minimal use of graphics, resulting in very plain, unprofessional-looking sites without the extras that a paid host provides. Finally, your URL will be long and clearly indicative of the fact that you are operating from a free site, which does little to inspire confidence in your customers.

A good web host doesn't have to be expensive. There are a lot of good, affordable hosting services out there; many provide packages that include a registered domain name, professionally-designed templates, secure services, e-mail boxes, online or phone support, and more. Web hosts can cost as little as $8 or as much as $100 per month, depending on your needs.

Domain Registration

The name of your web site should clearly and accurately reflect your business. It will be easier for customers to remember if it matches your eBay User ID or eBay Store name. Both Karen Kelley (eBay User ID: thepinkboutique) and Georgene Harkness (eBay User ID: mynewthreads) have matched their web addresses to their eBay User IDs and eBay Stores, which makes it easy for customers to find them.

Once you have registered your domain name, protect it by asking the registrar to "lock it" and prevent someone else from stealing and transferring it. Domain name theft is becoming increasingly common and is quite easy to do, so take steps to prevent it from happening to you.

Redirecting Visitors

Web forwarding is a service that allows you to send any visitor to your web site or to any other web page you designate. The service is available through most domain name registrars and hosting services. Both Harkness (www.mynewthreads.com) and Kelley (www.thepinkboutique.net), for example, have their sites set up so visitors are immediately sent to their respective eBay stores when their URLs are typed in. This can be particularly useful when the page you want visitors to see has a long, complicated URL. You can also avoid paying hosting fees by using a domain forwarding service if you have a domain name for your eBay store but don't want to actually build and maintain a separate web site.

Clear Visibility

To get the maximum benefit of a web site, you want it ranking as high as possible in the results when a user conducts an online search. One way to increase your site's visibility is to make it "bot-friendly." The term refers to the "robots" or "spiders" that search engines send crawling through the internet, scavenging information from web sites that are indexed for searches. The more information those electronic researchers can access from your site, the higher your ranking will be.

When people use a search engine to look for something specific, they search by keywords and phrases. Think about what keywords and phrases people you want to attract to your site might use, and place those words in meta tags, page title headings, and throughout the pages of your site for the crawlers to find.

Site maps are a very easy way for search engine bots to gather data. Every business web site should have a site map to make it easy for visitors and crawlers to access its pages. When creating your site map, use simple text links because crawlers often have trouble reading Java script, drop-down menus, and search boxes.

Another easy way to raise your site's search engine ranking is to swap reciprocal links. These are text links or banner ads that are exchanged with another web site owner. Many search engines track how many other sites point back to your site. The more sites that feature your business and URL, the higher your site will rank in search results. A similar technique to trading reciprocal links is to submit articles and other information to be published on other web sites with the stipulation your name and URL are included. For example, Liz Baker (eBay User ID: theliteratelady) regularly submits recipes to other web sites. When those sites publish her material, they include her name and URL, and that information is picked up by the search engines. Baker says her recipe site gets approximately 500 visitors a day and that traffic is primarily due to reciprocal links and using appropriate keywords. "This is a very simple site without any bells or whistles, but it seems to get a lot of activity. I trade links with other web sites and keep them listed on a separate web page. Although I initially started out asking other site owners to trade links with me, that trend has now reversed and almost every day I receive an e-mail from someone wanting to exchange links," she says. "It took almost two years to reach this point, but I'm glad I stuck with it, because it's definitely paying off."

You can also raise your site's visibility by submitting your site to all of the search engines (there are hundreds). You might want to hire a marketing specialist to take on this time-consuming task.

Affiliate Links

Affiliate programs (eBay's and others) not only generate easy revenue, they can also drive up your site's popularity and visibility. Choose your affiliate programs carefully, and make certain they are based on the interests of your target market. Then place appropriate graphics and links in strategic places throughout your site.

Privacy Policy

Junk e-mail and the risk of being a victim of online fraud may make some people reluctant to sign up for your newsletter or purchase products from your site. To allay these fears, have a clearly-written and prominently placed privacy policy that states both how you use and safeguard personal information.

The most effective privacy policies are short, to the point, in plain English (not legalese), easy to find, and easy to understand. For free assistance in composing a policy for your site, visit Web Dev Tips (www.webdevtips.com/web devtips/code-gen/privacy.shtml) and the Direct Marketing Association (www.the-dma. org/priva-cy/creating.shtml).

eBay's Tools to Help Market Your Auctions

eBay provides a wide range of services you can use to promote your auctions. Some are free; most are available for a nominal fee. Use these tools wisely; you don't want to end up paying $20 to list an item that will sell for $10.

An excellent eBay promotional option is the featured auction, which is given extra exposure in the "Featured" sections at the top of the listings pages. You can use a featured auction to attract buyers to your nonfeatured listings and boost sales of those items. It's an approach similar to the loss leaders grocery stores use: popular items are sold at cost or below just to generate traffic in the store.

Bob Bidwell (eBay User ID: plates-n-stuff) uses the featured option for category listings once or twice a week. "It is the cheapest form of advertising," he says. "If I put a featured auction in the Briar model horse category, it may get looked at 1,000 times or more. Then hopefully 100 of those people will go on to look at my other auctions."

You can use different feature options, depending on what is most appropriate for your products. A Featured Plus! auction gets stand-out placement in both category and keyword search results. Gallery Featured costs about the same, but fewer people search by gallery pictures than by list view, which limits your exposure.

A Home Page Featured auction gives you the highest visibility on eBay by rotating your listing in a special display on eBay's home page, as well as on eBay's browse hub page and in the special featured items section. If you try this option, carefully measure your results. Many eBay sellers have found that shoppers often skip past the Home Page Featured auctions to go to a category or search results page for the specific items they want.

If you think your item would make a good gift, use eBay's Gift Services feature to have the gift icon (a wrapped package) appear next to your listing on search and browse pages. That tells buyers you offer gift services, such as gift-wrapping, gift cards, express shipping, and shipping directly to the gift recipient. Include details of and charges for the gift services you provide in your auction description. Most of the sellers we talked to did not find this feature valuable; however, as eBay continues to promote the site to buyers, you may get some seasonal benefits from promoting your items as possible gifts.

eBay Keywords

eBay Keywords is a service offered by adMarketplace that offers sellers the ability to place advertisements for their eBay store or products above the usual eBay listings in the form of a banner ad or text box. AdMarketplace is a transparent, auction-based, pay-per-click system that allows sellers to decide how much they are willing to pay-per-click per keyword.

It works like this: You bid the maximum cost-per-click (CPC) that you are willing to pay when a user clicks on your ad. After you submit your bid, adMarketplace ranks your ad in the ad rotation relative to what the maximum CPC bid is for others in the system. The higher your CPC bid, the higher your ad is ranked in the ad rotation for the selected keyword and the greater the likelihood your ad will be shown first to an eBay shopper. To learn more about eBay keywords and to sign up, visit www.ebaykeywords.com or www.admarketplace.net.

Your ad should be appealing and targeted to your market. You don't have to pay unless someone clicks on your ad—but you do have to pay for every click, whether or not the shopper makes a purchase. Karen Kelley hired a graphic designer to create a striking logo specifically for her eBay business, and she uses it in her eBay Keywords ads. The drawback is that she gets a lot of clicks from people who don't buy—clicks she has to pay for. "My logo banner looks so cool, so people always click on it," she says.

Cross-Promote Your Auctions

Promote your other auctions and store merchandise in every auction. Even though eBay provides a link at the top of each auction listing to "view seller's other items," this may be overlooked unless you give the buyer a reason to click on it.

Cross-promote by letting prospective bidders know you are offering similar or complementary items. For instance, if you are selling a red skirt in one auction, let shoppers know you have a coordinating jacket or belt available in another auction. As an extra incentive, offer combined shipping on multiple purchases. eBay offers a cross-promoting feature that automatically displays some of your other items when someone places a bid or wins one of your auctions. You can choose which items are cross-promoted or let eBay do it for you.

Signature Lines

One of the easiest, most cost-efficient ways to promote yourself on the internet is through direct links in your signature lines. Though it is one of the most effective means of promoting your auctions, this simple marketing technique is often overlooked. Generally, signature lines are an acceptable form of discreet marketing and are not considered spam because they appear at the bottom of your message.

Kathy Logan (eBay User ID: rosie_peachstate) says that using her signature lines when she posts messages on discussion forums is like using a cyber-billboard: It's there for everyone to see. "I will put in some kind of a teaser, such as 'pewter embellishment' or 'pewter accents,' and people will wonder what I'm selling and click the link," she says. "Most of my trade comes from posting on discussion groups because of my signature links."

Signature lines should be short—no more than three or four lines, including the URL. You may want to create different signature lines for different purposes—perhaps one for your personal e-mail, another for your business e-mail, and others for posting on discussion forums and e-mail discussion lists. Update and modify your signatures frequently so viewers who see them on a regular basis won't be inclined to overlook them. Use them to promote free shipping or a specialty item. Or attract attention with funny or motivational quotes that are changed every week. Logan says she often adds a humorous tag line, which gets attention.

Shipping Inserts

To generate repeat business and be memorable in your customers' minds, include a shipping insert in every package you send out. Such inserts can range from a thank-you card, flier, brochure, newsletter, discount coupon, or anything else that promotes your company. (See Figure 11.1 on page 138.) Some eBay sellers use greeting cards appropriate for the season or even small pieces of candy as an insert. You might even consider investing in small promotional items, such as pens, calendars, or magnets, printed with your User ID, eBay Store, or web site. Be sure whatever you choose is light enough that it will not increase your shipping costs.

Logan adds a surprise to every package she sends out. Many of her customers make collages or scrapbooks, so she might insert a strip of ticket stubs or a few playing cards as a gift. "Just a little something they might be able to use somewhere down the line. It doesn't really matter what it is," she says. "People just like to get a little bonus. It makes them feel special."

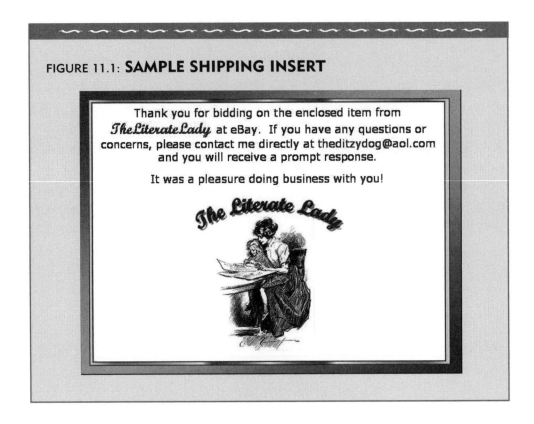

FIGURE 11.1: **SAMPLE SHIPPING INSERT**

Thank you for bidding on the enclosed item from
The Literate Lady at eBay. If you have any questions or
concerns, please contact me directly at theditzydog@aol.com
and you will receive a prompt response.

It was a pleasure doing business with you!

Newsletters and Promotional E-Mails

Offer a free e-newsletter with information related to your product line. In addition
to articles, use the newsletter to promote your current auctions. You can also
include affiliate links to other eBay auctions or third-party programs.

Don't make your newsletter an ill-disguised sales brochure. The content does
not have to be lengthy, but it should be solid and relevant. If you send your subscribers
junk, they'll unsubscribe. From your auction listing, direct interested subscribers to
your About Me page to sign up for your newsletter. Entice new subscribers by
offering a bonus such as an informational e-book. Retain subscribers by holding a
monthly drawing for a prize (ideally a promotional item that matches your product
line).

You may also want to send out other types of promotional e-mails. eBay prohibits members from sending unsolicited or unwanted e-mail, but you can extend an invitation for interested parties to sign up for your mailing list. In your auction descriptions, include a note that directs people to your About Me page where they will find a subscription link. It's also effective to provide a subscription link in your follow-up e-mails after the auction has closed.

Your promotional e-mails need to be sent out often enough to keep your customers interested and not so often that you annoy them. Let your customers know when they sign up how often they can expect to hear from you. For example, one eBay seller sends out a weekly e-mail listing all her new auctions. Another has developed his own software that sends a daily e-mail with links to auctions that are closing in a few hours at prices below the seller's cost. This, by the way, is a very clever marketing technique, because customers feel like they've got an inside track on bargains and when they bid on items they may not otherwise buy, they are driving up the final sale prices.

Just as you need a privacy policy for your web site, you also need one for the mailing lists you develop. Include a statement on your subscription invitation that says: "We value your privacy and do not take your trust for granted. We will never sell, share, or lease your name, e-mail address, or other information with anyone." Each e-mail you send should have a link to allow the recipient to unsubscribe.

Though it's possible to manage an e-mail list manually, it's far more efficient to automate. eBay Store owners can build up to five different mailing lists for free. The different lists let you send targeted mailings to your customers.

To set up a list outside of eBay, use an autoresponder service. Many are free through discussion list forums, such as Yahoo! Groups or Topica. Others are available through monthly subscription services, such as Constant Contact (www.con stantcontact.com) or Aweber (www.aweber.com) that come with professional templates, HTML features, and are ad free.

Advertising

Very few eBay sellers advertise their auctions or stores outside of eBay, but it's an investment worth considering, especially if you have high-ticket, high-margin items to sell. Because eBay's market is virtually worldwide, choose publications with a national or even international circulation. You may, for example, want to run a small classified or display ad in newspapers such as *The New York Times, The*

Wall Street Journal, or *USA Today*. Another approach is to use niche publications that match your product line, such as *Golf Monthly* if you sell golfing equipment or *Doll World* if you sell collectible dolls. You may also benefit from advertising in online newsletters and e-zines that target your market.

If you're going to spend the money to advertise, track your results. One way is to offer customers responding to the ad a discount on shipping if they tell you they saw your ad or provide a code you included in the ad.

The Federal Trade Commission (FTC) regulates advertising content to prevent deceptive and unfair acts and practices. All of your ads (including your auction and store item descriptions) must be truthful, not misleading, and any claims must be substantiated. If you are selling goods you obtain from a manufacturer or distributor, ask for material to back up claims before you repeat what the manufacturer says about the product. Should the manufacturer fail to provide proof or give you something that looks questionable, be very cautious about proceeding. If your advertisements fail to comply with the law, you could face enforcement actions or civil lawsuits.

Gift Certificates

When you have an eBay store, gift certificates can work as a customer reward and retention tool, as well as a way to acquire new customers. For example, you may set up a rewards program and give a gift certificate of $5 for every $100 your customers spend in your eBay store during a particular month (or other specified time period). You can also encourage your existing customers to buy gift certificates as presents.

Assign a code number to each certificate, and keep track of the name of the customer, date of purchase, amount, and when the certificate was redeemed. Though buyers generally like to have a physical certificate, you don't need to require they send you that piece of paper to redeem the certificate; they can do it with their code number when they make a purchase.

There are several gift certificate templates available online at sites such as Microsoft Office Online (www.office.microsoft.com) or KoolPrint (www.koolprint. com), or you can create your own using MS Word, Printmaster, or similar software. When you issue a certificate, complete the form, and save it as a .JPG or .PDF file

FIGURE 11.2: **SAMPLE GIFT CERTIFICATE**

so it cannot be tampered with. You can e-mail the file or mail a hard copy to your customer. See the example in Figure 11.2.

Don't confuse your own store gift certificate with eBay's gift certificates, which allow the shopper to buy from any eBay seller. eBay's gift certificates are a great tool to attract more buyers to the site, but not necessarily to your store or auctions.

Seasonal Promotions

Just as the world of brick-and-mortar retailing experiences seasonal fluctuations in sales patterns, so does eBay. If your products are seasonal or if you can create a seasonal marketing hook, take advantage of recognized consumer buying patterns. Don't just focus on the big holidays, such as Christmas and Easter. Build promotions around Valentine's Day, St. Patrick's Day, Mother's Day, Father's Day, start of summer, Independence Day, back to school, Labor Day, Grandparents' Day, Halloween, and more.

Logistics force major retailers to stock seasonal merchandise well in advance of when those items are likely to be used—that's why you see bathing suits in stores in February and winter coats on display in August. Your promotions can be more timely—in fact, the closer to the promotional event itself, the higher the price you're likely to get. People who shop on eBay for Halloween items in the spring are looking for bargains; they'll pay more in October for the same items.

When you're coming down to the wire with a holiday promotion, use shorter duration auctions with a Buy It Now price to allow last-minute shoppers to make an immediate purchase.

Word of Mouth

The most powerful form of marketing is word of mouth. Build a team of supporters by encouraging your family members, friends, associates, and non-eBay customers to check out your auctions and visit your eBay store so they can help spread the word about your eBay business. If you're offering quality merchandise, your supporters will be happy to help.

Publicity and Public Relations

Publicity and public relations can be very powerful marketing tools and—like advertising—most eBay sellers fail to take advantage of these tools. The exposure can generate significant business. Whenever QuikDrop gets featured on local television or in the newspaper, the store fills up with merchandise to sell, says Fred Johnson, the franchise's area developer in Central Florida.

Publicity is the process of getting yourself, your company, or your product mentioned in a print or broadcast story. You do not pay for this coverage, nor do you have any control over what the reporter ultimately says—a sharp contrast to advertising, where you buy the space and control exactly what goes in it. A big risk involved in publicity is that a reporter may not understand your business or may for whatever reason portray you in a negative light. Negate this risk by always answering reporters' calls and questions promptly and completely, and by providing written information that clearly explains your operation. Some newspapers, especially smaller ones, will publish prewritten news releases or publicity stories; this lets you be sure the information is accurate. If you have the opportunity to participate in a broadcast interview, practice ahead of time so you will appear smooth and polished.

Public relations includes publicity but is a broader issue that encompasses such efforts as image, investor relations, crisis communications, special events, community relations, and other activities that influence how the public perceives you and your company.

Because eBay itself is a huge, multinational corporation, it is routinely covered in the business media. The company has a substantial internal PR department and also contracts with outside agencies to get the eBay message out. That's good for eBay the company, and all eBay sellers, because it attracts new users who may be customers for you.

What will be of greater value to you is the publicity you generate yourself about your particular business. When you do something that's newsworthy, issue a release to your local media outlets and any other publications and broadcast sources prospective customers might be reading, watching, or listening to. When you add a product line, expand your services, reach a certain sales goal, or hire new people, issue a news release.

When something happens on a national level that relates to what you do or the types of merchandise you sell, write up a media advisory with a local spin. Say you're a trading assistant or have a trading post, and someone puts up an unusual or even bizarre item for auction that catches the attention of national reporters. Immediately contact your local journalists, present yourself as an eBay expert (which you are), and offer to answer any questions they may have or tell them about some of the unusual items you've handled for your clients.

It's important to note that when these unusual items that are up for auction hit the headlines, it's because eBay users put the word out. eBay's corporate public relations department does not promote individual auctions.

Trade Shows

Trade shows can be a valuable resource for eBay sellers from a variety of angles. Shows provide a venue for you to find merchandise you can sell on eBay, make contacts with wholesalers and other business product and service providers, learn more about running your business, and market your own products.

There are two types of shows: consumer, which focus on home, garden, and other consumer themes, and business-to-business, in which exhibitors market their products and services to other companies. You can likely benefit by attending, and perhaps even exhibiting, in both.

For example, do you sell products that appeal to women? Consider exhibiting in one of the Southern Women's Shows (www.southernshows.com). Thousands of prospective customers can see your merchandise on display and either purchase there or visit you on eBay later to buy. In the jewelry business? At the Chicago Jewelry, Fashion, and Accessories Show (www.transworldexhibits.com), you can sell your own products and also find additional merchandise to auction and stock in your store. Find trade shows scheduled throughout the country at *Tradeshow Week Online* (www.tradeshowweek.com) or Tradeshow News Network (www.tsnn.com).

To get comfortable with trade shows, start by attending some local ones. Your local chamber of commerce or convention center can provide you with a show calendar. Wear comfortable shoes, take a generous supply of business cards, and walk up and down every aisle, looking at every booth. Analyze which displays are effective and which ones aren't. Talk to salespeople. Find out about their products, and ask how the show is working for them. And if you're tempted to make a purchase, consider what the salesperson is doing that appeals to you. Many show exhibitors collect business cards for follow-up sales efforts. Leave your card when asked so you can see what type of marketing the exhibitor does and if those techniques can be adapted to your business.

When you're ready to exhibit, identify shows that will be attended by your potential customers. You're not likely to sell too many hunting knives at a show targeting expectant mothers—but if you sell baby furniture, that's a good place to exhibit. Show sponsors will be able to estimate the total number of attendees and give you demographics so you can tell if they fit your target-market profile. Also, not all shows allow retail sales on the exhibit floor. Find out if the show you're considering does so you can plan your display and bring sufficient inventory.

The setup of your booth should be as thoughtfully and carefully planned as an in-store display or a web site. Your exhibit does not need to be elaborate or expensive, but it does need to be professional and inviting. If you're going to stock your booth with merchandise to sell, avoid cramming it so full it looks cluttered. Find out if there is an area outside the exhibit hall where you can store excess inventory until you need it.

Never leave your booth unattended during exhibit hours. Not only is it a security risk because someone could walk off with valuable merchandise when you're not there, but you could also miss a tremendous sales opportunity. Even if you're a one-person operation, find someone who can work the show with you so you can take breaks during the day.

Consider some sort of giveaway item such as a pen, mug, or notepad imprinted with your company name and eBay User ID. Do not display these items openly or pass them out indiscriminately. Store them discreetly out of sight, and present them as appropriate to prospective customers. You can be more generous with brochures and business cards, but keep in mind that most of this literature will find its way to the trash can within hours of the show's closing. Ask visitors to your booth to sign up for an e-mail newsletter or special promotions mailing list so you can contact them later.

Write It Down and Take Action

Thinking that all you have to do to have a successful business selling on eBay is to find things you can buy for practically nothing and sell for huge profits is a serious mistake. No matter what your product or potential profit margin is, you need to promote your auctions and your business through marketing. Once you've considered your various options for marketing, put together a written marketing plan—and implement it. Figure 11.3 can help you get started.

FIGURE 11.3: **ASK YOURSELF**

To create your marketing plan, start by answering these questions:

• Exactly what is my business? _____

_____

FIGURE 11.3: **ASK YOURSELF**, continued

- Who are my customers? Where are they located? _____

_____

- How much can I expect an average customer to buy from me in one year? _____

_____

- What do I provide my customers? _____

_____

- Who is my competition? (Other eBay sellers, brick-and-mortar retailers, online retailers, etc.) _____

_____

- Why would my customers buy from me instead of someone else? _____

_____

- How can I best communicate with my customers? (Print advertising, newsletters, e-mail, web site, etc.) _____

_____

- What marketing techniques are likely to be most effective in reaching my target market? _____

_____

- What is unique about my product? _____

_____

FIGURE 11.3: **ASK YOURSELF**, continued

- How will trends affect the product I'm marketing? _____

  _____

- What is the projected size of my targeted market? _____

  _____

- How can I attract new customers and keep existing ones? _____

  _____

CHAPTER 12

Add Revenue with eBay Subsidiaries

IN ADDITION TO SELLING MERCHANDISE on eBay through auctions or store listings, you can generate significant revenue utilizing programs available through eBay subsidiaries, such as PayPal, Half.com, and Elance. Some of these subsidiaries offer additional selling venues; others can generate referral income. Look carefully to see what each program offers and how you can use these resources for greater profits.

Get Paid by PayPal Merchant Referral Program

PayPal is widely known as one of the most popular internet intermediary money exchange services. What is not quite so well known is that it has a merchant affiliate program that pays quite handsomely. You can earn up to $1,000 (based on .5 percent of the merchant's non-eBay revenue) for referring new business merchants to sign up for a business or premier account with PayPal.

Consider this: By signing up only one business merchant a month, you could make as much as $12,000 a year without selling—or shipping—anything. Currently, PayPal does not limit the number of merchant accounts on which you can earn a commission.

Referrals must come through web site and newsletter links, or an e-mail to someone with whom you have a pre-existing relationship. PayPal strictly forbids recruiting new merchant accounts through spamming and unsolicited e-mail.

Use the concepts in Chapters 11 and 13 to put together a targeted marketing plan to launch this program. PayPal will provide you with the tools, banners, and buttons you need to get started. Just log into your PayPal account and click the "Refer Merchants" link in the What's New box of your account overview.

Half.com Meets You Halfway

Half.com is a fixed-price online marketplace for books, movies, games, CDs, DVDs, and electronic equipment. Buyers are able to make purchases immediately using a major credit card.

Half.com's appeal is that it bypasses the auction process and allows purchases to be made immediately for a specified price. When you list on Half.com, follow the same research process you would for an eBay auction. Check to see how many similar and identical items are up for sale and at what price. You'll also need to rate the quality of your items, from brand new to unacceptable (although you cannot actually sell unacceptable quality items). If you are unsure of how to price an item, Half.com will make a recommendation.

Buyers search by keyword or category. When they look at a specific item, a single page comes up with a description of the product, followed by a list of all the sellers who are offering it. Items are sorted first by quality then by price. A "like new" music CD with the lowest price will show up at the top of the second group after "brand new" items. The search results also show your shipping method. Allow space for a brief comment about the product, such as "CD was played only once and has no scratches," and include a link for more information.

Half.com features some great buyers' tools that also benefit sellers. The wish list allows buyers to keep track of items they want but that are not in stock. When an item becomes available, Half.com sends an e-mail notifying the buyer. The pre-ordering tool lets buyers tell Half.com exactly what they want to buy, and that item is automatically purchased when it becomes available. Also, if a searched item is not available on Half.com, browsers are notified of matches on eBay.

You must register with Half.com even if you are already an eBay user. However, you can use the same eBay User ID and password, and all your feedback ratings and comments for both sites will be combined and visible to eBay and Half.com shoppers. If you are not an eBay user and register on Half.com, you will be automatically registered on eBay with the same User ID and password.

Half.com requires a valid credit card to sign up as either a buyer or seller. Sellers are paid through direct deposit or printed checks on a pre-established schedule. Printed checks are cut twice a month for sellers with a balance of $50 or more; checks are cut once a month for sellers with a balance under $50. Direct deposit payments are made twice a month regardless of the balance.

Half.com does not charge listing fees but does collect a commission when items are sold. Sellers receive a flat shipping credit for each sale; the amount is determined by Half.com based on the product and type of shipping method used. You must always offer U.S. Postal Service Media Mail. Whether you offer additional shipping options is up to you, but it's a good idea to give buyers a choice between the slower mail service and expedited shipping alternatives.

Products remain in your inventory until they are sold or you remove them. When a sale is made, Half.com notifies you by e-mail and asks you to confirm shipment. They notify the buyer when the item is on the way.

Buyer-seller interaction is minimal and usually occurs only if the buyer has a specific question about your item. Even so, you can encourage repeat business with great service, along with a package insert or a follow-up e-mail.

Half.com's affiliate program for webmasters and newsletter publishers pays $5 to $9 for new customer referrals. Like eBay, Half.com has teamed with Commission Junction, a third-party affiliate program. See Chapter 13 for more on affiliate programs.

Freelance at Elance

Want to do business online but don't want to sell tangible merchandise? Elance Online is your solution. This eBay subsidiary is an excellent venue for individuals and companies to subcontract work projects to freelance service providers in a variety of fields, including writing, translation, administrative support, web site development, legal services, software, technology, architecture, engineering, graphic design, and more.

Cynthia Bull (Elance User ID: cynrje) discovered Elance while browsing around eBay. She says, "I've found Elance to be an exceptional employment resource. It allows you to do something you really enjoy and are good at." Bull started doing transcription work, then expanded her services to include writing and editing and eventually phased out transcription. The experience and connections she made through Elance allowed her to establish and expand an online business independent of eBay.

Here's how Elance works: Clients post their job descriptions with deadlines, budgets, experience requirements, and other considerations. Projects are screened and must meet Elance's Project Posting Guidelines that are found in the Buyer's Help section. In addition to outlining a number of procedures, the guidelines prohibit the posting of adult-related content or businesses, projects that offer commissions or fee-based compensation, or anything related to bulk e-mail or spam. Service providers bid on the project, and the client makes a decision based on a combination of price and qualifications.

If you bid on an Elance project, completely address all the issues the client has included in the job description. Indicate that you clearly understand the scope of the project as you present your own knowledge and expertise.

"Make your presentation as professional as you can," Bull advises. "Be willing to share who you are, your ethics and experience, and not just what you can do. Buyers frequently want to know *who* they're dealing with as much as the services the provider will give them." Of course, a competitive price is always an advantage, but it's not always the client's primary consideration. And with the right skills and expertise, you can justify a higher fee.

As with eBay, Elance uses a public feedback system for performance reviews. At the conclusion of an assignment, the client is asked to rate the provider's performance in several areas on a scale of one to five, with five being the best. Certainly the more positive feedback you have, the greater your first impression is. However, new providers with limited feedback are not necessarily at a disadvantage when placing bids alongside seasoned providers, because often clients are looking for a fresh perspective and new energy.

Clients and providers must register with a valid credit card; however, Elance does not charge clients. Service providers pay a monthly subscription fee based on category and provider level; this fee is discounted if paid quarterly or annually. In addition, providers are charged a transaction fee when the assignment is completed. Consider these fees a cost of doing business, much as you would rent and marketing costs, and keep the transaction fee in mind when setting your prices. Bull says that serious Elance providers can quickly and easily recoup the subscription fee with just one or two assignments. "It just depends on the amount of work you do," she says. "You need to think about how serious you are going to be about being an Elance provider."

Elance Online has a free affiliate program open to anyone, not just clients and service providers, and pays a range of commissions for new users. You'll receive tools to assist you in promoting their services.

Take a Load Off with PayLoadz

As digitally downloadable products, such as music, software, videos, and e-books are growing in popularity, so are entrepreneurial opportunities for internet suppliers. Increasingly, consumers want instant gratification by being able to browse, click, pay, and receive the digital object of their desire within minutes of discovering it.

PayLoadz is a fully automated system that delivers digital products for immediate download. Although it is not an eBay subsidiary, the operation uses PayPal's online payment system exclusively and interfaces with eBay to such a degree that we felt it was appropriate to include PayLoadz in this chapter.

Use PayLoadz to sell your digital goods on your own site, on auction sites, and in the PayLoadz e-store. For example, if you set up a fixed-price auction for an e-book, PayLoadz gives you an auction code to be placed in the listing title. When an auction purchase is made, eBay immediately directs the buyer to PayPal. When payment is made, PayPal notifies PayLoadz to send downloading instructions. Because the system is automated, this all happens in seconds. Keep in mind that eBay has strict guidelines about the sale and distribution of digitally downloadable products. You must be the owner of the material or an authorized reseller and state that fact in your auction description.

The process is similar when a customer makes a purchase directly from your web site or through an e-mail link: She is immediately sent to PayPal's checkout, and when payment is made, she receives downloading instructions from PayLoadz.

Liz Baker (eBay User ID theliteratelady) uses PayLoadz to process orders on digital eCookbooks. "PayLoadz has been a wonderful vehicle to promote and download digital products on my web site, in newsletters, and through eBay auctions, whether the products are my own or I'm functioning as an affiliate," she says. "The interface with PayPal and eBay makes the entire process simple and profitable." A PayLoadz basic account is free if your monthly transactions do not exceed $250. Higher volume sellers can choose from a range of fee-based account options.

Though having your own web site or newsletter will enhance your sales, you do not need either to use PayLoadz. As well as auctions, you can place items in the PayLoadz e-store or allow other merchants to sell your product through the affiliate builder program. You can also use that same affiliate program to sell products of other PayLoadz members on your web site and in your newsletters. In addition, PayLoadz has a referral program that pays commissions for new users.

Creating a new account is extremely easy. You just need to enter your e-mail address and assign a password. After doing that, you will be taken to a page where you can set up your preferences for future sales, and you'll be ready to go. You will not be asked for a credit card or other financial information unless your sales transactions exceed $250 or you need additional storage space for your digital products. When that happens, PayLoadz will send you an e-mail asking you to upgrade your account at your earliest convenience.

The Door of Opportunity Is Open

Savvy online operators are making extraordinary incomes by taking advantage of these types of opportunities—and you can, too, whether you use an affiliate program to enhance your existing business or build your business around an affiliate program. Of course, like anything worth doing, it takes work to see results. Take your time, do your research, and make yourself comfortable with the program of your choice.

CHAPTER 13

Make Money on eBay without Selling Anything

BAY'S AFFILIATE PROGRAM ALLOWS YOU to earn commissions simply by refer-
ring people to eBay auction listings—they don't have to be yours, and you
don't have to sell a thing! You don't even have to have a web site. All you
need is a computer, credit card, time, and imagination. As an affiliate, you
can promote other people's auctions without having to worry about keeping
inventory, collecting payments, or shipping items. With millions of viewers access-
ing eBay each month, you can tap into this phenomenal enterprise by sending
them to specific landing pages for the bargains they are looking for.

eBay offers their affiliates a two-tier program that has a range of commissions
for recruiting new users, as well as generating bids from previously registered
users. Like most sales programs, the more activity, the higher the commission, so
your revenue will depend on the number of registrants and bidders referred by
you.

A newly registered active member is someone who registers by using your referral link and then either places a bid on an auction (they don't actually have to win the auction) or uses the Buy It Now (BIN) feature within 30 days of registering. A previously registered member is someone who already has an eBay user ID, but bids on an auction or purchases a BIN by using your referral link.

Affiliate Registration Process

Registering with the eBay affiliate program is free and easy through Commission Junction. Access the affiliate program through the links found on eBay's site map or at the bottom of the home page. From there you will learn more about the program, including payment structure, requirements for commissions, and the clever, innovative tools eBay has designed for affiliates.

During the affiliate sign-up process you will be redirected to Commission Junction's registration form and asked to provide a URL to your web site and/or a name for your newsletter. Most affiliate programs require you to have a web site and provide a URL so they can verify your business meets their guidelines. Commission Junction will allow you to participate in the program if you publish a newsletter but do not have a web site.

Once you have completed your registration with Commission Junction, you can take advantage of thousands of other affiliate programs (in addition to eBay) whose products and services you can promote and advertise. You must log in at least every 30 days to keep your account active with Commission Junction, otherwise it will be deactivated and you will have to go through the sign-up process again. Although CJ's help section is somewhat limited, eBay offers a lot of advice on its affiliate pages to help you make the most of its affiliate program. eBay wants you to succeed, because when affiliates make money, everyone is making money.

Getting Started

eBay provides affiliates with all of the necessary promotional and marketing tools, including hundreds of banners, logos, and buttons, as well as creative text links to use in different marketing campaigns.

Use the Flexible Destination Tool to generate trackable links to any of eBay's search or auction pages. The links only take a few seconds to create. You will be given the opportunity to use specific eBay banners or creative text ads that can be used on web sites, in newsletters, for online classified ads, or in pay-per-click ads. For instance, if you wanted to promote auctions for vintage Tupperware, you would enter the words "vintage Tupperware" in the eBay search box. This will take you to a landing page that will show all of the current auctions for this item. Copy the link shown in your browser and paste it in the designated box of the Flexible Destination Tool. Then enter your Commission Junction affiliate number and the text you would like users to click (e.g., *Click here for vintage Tupperware*)—and *presto!* you will immediately be provided with HTML code that can be used in your marketing campaigns.

Liz Baker (eBay User ID: theliteratelady) is an avid eBay buyer who started using the eBay affiliate program to help support her shopping habit. After receiving a couple of commission checks from eBay, she decided this was a much more enjoyable and profitable venture and turned her new hobby into a part-time job. She has a recipe site that also features a monthly newsletter, so she is able to get a lot of exposure for her affiliate links. "A lot of my newsletter subscribers are interested in vintage and church cookbooks, so each month I have special features about eBay auctions. I'll send people to either a landing page that lists a selection of church cookbooks, or to an auction that is selling a really good vintage cookbook," she says. "It doesn't matter how inexpensive the item is being sold for because my commission is not based on a percentage of the sales. It's based on how many users sign up and place bids."

The tool for Dynamic Landing Pages also provides links to specific landing pages for popular items that have organized categories to make a visitor's search easier. This tool is useful when promoting items, such as NASCAR merchandise, that have hundreds of categories and hundreds of current auctions within each of those categories.

You can also show current eBay auctions on any web page by using the Editor Kit that can customize listing details and product information. This is done by using specific keywords of your choice, seller IDs, category IDs, or a combination of any of these. You can even specify a price range. In addition, a variety of display options are available in a style that will best compliment your site. This means you can add real-time auctions to your web site that are relevant to its content. For instance, if you have a camping or fishing site, you can display eBay auctions for camping or fishing gear. If the bulk of your visitors tend to be budget conscious, set parameters so that only auctions selling items under $50, $25, or less are shown.

Baker uses the Editor Kit to show live eBay listings on her recipe site. On the home page, which gets the most hits or views, she features auctions that are selling kitchenware items. On her main recipe page, which also receives a large number of visitors, she displays auctions listing only new and used cookbooks under $10.

Hot Topics and Current Trends

Even if you already know what types of auctions you want to promote, you'll be able to maximize your affiliate marketing efforts if you know the current hot topics and trends. For example, a few years ago, sellers couldn't keep Beanie Babies in stock and were getting top dollar for the ones they had. But the popularity of—and the demand for—the floppy stuffed critters has declined sharply, which means links to Beanie Baby® auctions aren't likely to get a lot of hits. On the other hand, the *Bible* has consistently remained in the top 25 searched-for terms in the last year, along with dieting and finding baby names. Links to eBay landing pages that feature the *Bible* and products related to dieting and finding baby names are likely to get plenty of clicks.

Researching current trends and hot topics is easy with the following online tools.

WHAT'S HOT AT EBAY'S SELLER CENTRAL
(HTTP://PAGES.EBAY.COM/SELLERCENTRAL/WHATSHOT.HTML)
In addition to telling you what products are currently in demand, eBay also provides links to sections that have predictions of upcoming seasonal trends as well as dates that specific categories are going to be featured on the eBay home page.

WORDTRACKER (WWW.WORDTRACKER.COM)
This site has a ticker on the home page that shows the top 50 terms that were searched for during the past 24 hours. This information is updated daily and is free to the public. You can also subscribe to a free keyword weekly report that includes 500 of the most frequently searched keywords, including misspellings.

YAHOO! BUZZ INDEX (HTTP://BUZZ.YAHOO.COM/)
Find out what Yahoo! users are searching for, plus see articles on trends and hot topics.

LYCOS 50 DAILY REPORT (HTTP://50.LYCOS.COM/)
Check this site for the top 50 keyword searches conducted on Lycos the previous week. The Greatest Hits section includes articles and predictions on trends.

ASK JEEVES IQ INTERESTING QUERIES
(HTTP://SP.ASK.COM/DOCS/ABOUT/JEEVESIQ.HTML)
This page provides a weekly recap of the most popular search terms on AskJeeves.com.

WEBMASTER TOOLKIT—KEYWORD RESEARCH TOOL
(WWW.WEBMASTER-TOOLKIT.COM/KEYWORD-RESEARCH-TOOL.SHTML)
This is a webmaster's resource that can help you research words and phrases while specifying a search engine of your choice.

Making the Most of Affiliate Links with Google AdWords

Though you do not have to have a web site or newsletter to be an eBay affiliate, the reality is that the more you promote your links, the higher you raise their visibility, and the more likely you are to sign up new eBay users. An effective way to do that is with Google AdWords.

If you've ever done a Google search, you've seen AdWords. They are generated whenever someone browsing on the internet conducts a keyword search. AdWords appear as the sponsor links that are displayed at the top or on the side of a search results page.

Whenever an ad pops up in a keyword search and a browser clicks the link, the affiliate is charged a preselected amount of anywhere from five cents to several dollars. The affiliate decides in advance how much he is willing to pay per click. The placement of the ad in search page results will be determined by the popularity of the word or phrase and how much is paid per click.

Used correctly, AdWords can be one of the fastest methods to bring visitors to an eBay affiliate landing page of your choice. The challenge is finding out how to get the most exposure for the least amount of money and then to get a return on your investment. Not only do you want clickable ads with high visibility, you also want potential customers to be interested enough to register or bid on an auction they found through your affiliate link. Choosing appropriate keywords is critical.

For example, if you want to send visitors to a landing page for books on baby names that are up for auction, don't purchase the words "baby" or "babies" by themselves. Those words will generate a lot of impressions and clicks, but when the visitor goes to that page and sees this is not what she was looking for, she will immediately click out of that page. The keywords you may have better results with are "baby name books" or "books on baby names."

To get started, use keyword lists to determine what the hot topics on the internet currently are. Choose a word or phrase, and type it into the search box at eBay. If the results turn up hundreds of items, restructure your search by narrowing the field to a more targeted search. For instance, if you enter "Halloween Costumes," you will get a landing page for hundreds of listed auctions for all ages and sizes. Your click-through-rate on a Google AdWord campaign will be high, but the return on prospective bidders and new registrants will be low as they will be frustrated trying to weed through the maze of auctions. The visitors will click out of that page before finding what they want, and this will ultimately cause you to lose money on your AdWord campaign.

Streamline the search criteria by entering "Halloween costumes for infants" or "girls Halloween costumes" so that when shoppers are referred to this page, they can quickly find what they are looking for. You may even want to narrow the search field even further by adding specific sizes. This will greatly increase the chance that browsers will want to register and/or bid on the relevant auctions.

As with an auction title, the headline of your AdWord needs to be eye-catching so browsers will be enticed to take a closer look. Only 25 character spaces are allowed in the title, so be creative. You will also be able to give a brief description. But with only 70 characters, make it compelling. Do this by making a call to action or outlining the benefits to the consumer, such as "Treat Yourself to Great Savings," "Brand Name Clothing at Bargain Basement Prices," or "Free Shipping on Select Items."

Google AdWords are just one of many ways to promote your eBay affiliate efforts and can easily be combined with the additional marketing ideas that were discussed in Chapter 11. No matter what type of business you have or products you are selling, being part of an affiliate program will increase your revenue by promoting merchandise or services that visitors to your site, subscribers to your newsletter, or surfers on the internet will be attracted to.

CHAPTER 14

Fundraising on eBay

SELLING ON EBAY IS A GREAT WAY TO make money for yourself. Buying and selling on eBay can also be a great way to raise funds for a good cause. In fact, as a community, eBay users are some of the most generous people in the world. Within days of the tsunami disaster in South Asia, eBay sellers were raising money for victims.

For years, individual sellers have used their own auctions as fundraisers for charities, but buyers had no way of knowing for sure if and how much of the profits were really going to the organization—or if the organization was legitimate.

The eBay Giving Works program responds to those issues by allowing sellers to clearly designate their donation amount and assuring buyers that the charity has been checked out. Sellers benefit in other ways:

- Listings are distinguished with the eBay Giving Works icon.
- Listings have increased search functionality.

- Buyer loyalty is enhanced by the alignment with a good cause.
- High final values are often generated because buyers will typically pay more for items that benefit a cause.
- Charitable contributions are managed in one place for tax deductions and other record-keeping.

eBay Giving Works

eBay has formed an alliance with MissionFish, a service of the Points of Light Foundation. MissionFish is a nonprofit auction expert, and the provider of the Giving Assistant, which is the listing tool for eBay Giving Works.

How It Works for eBay Sellers

Want all or a portion of your sales to go to your favorite charity? Here's how it works: The nonprofit organization must register with MissionFish as a beneficiary or recipient. The process is free. Then MissionFish verifies that the nonprofit is legitimate and places it in the MissionFish database. eBay sellers must also register with MissionFish. Again, there's no charge, but you need to get into the database.

When you decide to list an item to benefit a charity, you sign in at MissionFish and pick a nonprofit from the list. You select the percentage of the final value of the listing to donate (10 to 100 percent, with a $10 minimum). Complete your item listing, and submit it for the nonprofit's review.

The nonprofit has up to one business day to accept or decline participation in the listing. This step provides the nonprofits control over what businesses and products they are associated with. For example, an animal rights organization may prefer not to have a contribution made from the sale of a fur coat.

Once the nonprofit has accepted the listing, it goes up for sale on eBay either immediately or based on the seller's schedule, if specified. The item appears with the eBay Giving Works icon, and the benefiting nonprofit and the donation percentage also appear in the item description. The listing is displayed with all other eBay listings, as well as within the eBay Giving Works site and on the Nonprofit Homepage on MissionFish—so you get three listing venues for the price of one.

When the listing ends, all of the regular activities take place: the seller sends the buyer an invoice; the buyer pays; the seller acknowledges receipt of the payment and ships the merchandise. Then the seller makes the donation to MissionFish. If the seller doesn't pay the nonprofit by the second Monday after the auction ends, MissionFish collects the amount due from the seller's credit card. MissionFish holds the donation in escrow until the refund period expires (end of the month when the auction ends, plus a month, plus 15 days) to ensure the finality of the sale, and then distributes the funds, less a small processing fee, to the nonprofit and provides a receipt to the seller for the gift.

Nonprofits can also register as eBay sellers and then sign up with MissionFish to sell items on eBay to raise money.

Hold a Rummage Sale on eBay

You don't have to go through eBay Giving Works to sell for the benefit of a charity. Many Trading Assistants and Trading Posts offer programs to help local schools, churches, and other organizations raise money on eBay.

The church or garden club rummage sale that was once a staple of organizational fundraising is gradually disappearing due to lack of volunteers and other issues. But these groups still need to raise money, and many still have members who will donate valuable items to be sold. Fred Johnson, QuikDrop's Central Florida area developer, says all franchisees are trained to work with local nonprofits in fundraising programs that replace the traditional rummage sale.

The benefiting organization is asked to name one person as a coordinator to explain the program and assist with collecting items for sale. Depending on the organization's preferences, the items can be collected at a central location (such as the church, school, or clubhouse), and the local QuikDrop store will pick them up. Or items can be taken directly to the QuikDrop store, but the sellers must be sure to identify their items as a donation and for what specific charity or organization.

As with any seller, QuikDrop takes care of evaluating, photographing, and listing the items on eBay; collects payment; handles packing and shipping; and then sends the organization a check for the net proceeds of the sales and receipts to the donors so they can document their contribution. All normal selling policies apply, but QuikDrop's fees for fundraisers are discounted from their regular fees. As a Trading Assistant or a Trading Post, you can set your own policies for dealing with fundraisers.

The biggest challenge with this type of fundraising is weeding out the junk. Many people use charities as a place to dump their garbage, or they donate items that would typically sell for less than a dollar. As a middleperson, you can't make enough with that type of transaction on eBay to cover your costs and labor. QuikDrop's general policy is that items must be worth at least $50 on eBay. You would be wise to develop your own guidelines based on your operation.

Be sure to set a clear policy on what you will do if the item doesn't sell. Will you return it to the owner, the benefiting charity, or donate it to another charity that may be able to use it? You should also insist on taking possession of any items you are selling for charity on a consignment basis; don't risk running into a problem getting the item after the auction closes.

Keep the Giving Going

A significant benefit of selling on eBay to raise money for charities is that it doesn't have to be a one-time event, like the annual rummage sale or silent auction and dinner. You can set up an ongoing program that can be promoted throughout the year at the school, church, or other organization—which means that the charity gets regular revenue and you have a steady source of merchandise to sell on eBay. Explain to your nonprofit clients that they can have members donate things to sell at any time, not just on a specified date. The members can either contact you directly (in that case, they must be sure to specify what organization is benefiting), or the items can be collected through the organization. Help the nonprofit promote the concept to their membership with ads and fliers.

Cause Marketing

Increasingly, businesses are figuring out ways to do good works while promoting their own products and services—a technique known as cause marketing. It can allow you to build community goodwill, customer loyalty, and a stronger bond among your own employees, all at the same time.

Done correctly, cause marketing can create a win/win situation—but it can also be a double-edged sword that cuts swiftly and deeply. Before implementing a cause marketing program, consider these points:

- *Choose the cause carefully.* It's a good idea to avoid controversial issues. Instead, support a mainstream cause that isn't likely to offend anyone— there are plenty of them out there. Supporting a polarizing cause may attract some customers but may make others decide they wouldn't buy from you if their life depended on your product. If you do feel strongly about a divisive cause, support it on your own time and not in connection with your business.
- *Check out the agency.* If you're supporting an organization, be sure it's legitimate, well-run, and demonstrates a strong degree of accountability. If there's a problem with the agency or the people involved, even though your intentions are pure, you'll be tainted by association.
- *Be totally committed.* Embrace the cause thoroughly and completely. Just as enthusiasm is contagious, so is ambivalence. If you're not sincere, it will show.
- *Get your employees on board.* You set the example. If you're excited, your employees will be, too.
- *Promote and publicize your efforts.* Make people aware of what you're doing with signs in your facility (even if customers rarely come in—your employees and suppliers will see the signs), and put notes in all of your other promotional materials. Make the cause visible, but discreet. Don't make it look as though you're using the cause to promote your own agenda.
- *Keep good records.* This is important from a tax and general business perspective, as well as in case someone wants to see evidence that you're keeping your word. Always be able to show how much money went to the cause.

The bottom line on cause marketing is that it works. It's an effective way to have a positive impact on your community, improve your public image and customer relations, strengthen the bonds between you and your employees, and even grow your own business—although that shouldn't be your primary motivation. Doing the right thing for the right reasons will come back to you in a positive way.

CHAPTER 15

Managing the Money: From Zero to Millions

H OW YOU HANDLE THE MONEY YOU make from your eBay operation is the best indicator of how serious you are about your business. And if you're serious about your business, you need to be serious about the money. There are two sides to the issue of money:

1. How much you need to start and operate.
2. How much you can expect to take in.

Everything else involved in financial management falls under these two issues.

Many eBay sellers could rightfully be called "accidental business owners" because they started selling on eBay as a lark, using equipment and inventory they already owned, without any real thought of the future. If you're treating your eBay sales as entertainment that happens to generate a little extra money, this approach is fine. After all, selling on eBay is fun. But if your goal is to build an operation that will support you, your family, and maybe even some employees, you need to be prepared to deal with start-up economics, ongoing financial management, and strong record-keeping.

How Much Money Do You Need?

It takes very little cash to start selling things on eBay, especially if you already have a business and are simply adding another sales venue or if you start by selling things you already own. However, when you purchase inventory, and certainly as you grow, you'll need money to invest in inventory, facilities, services, and more sophisticated equipment.

The typical eBay seller starts with very little capital and uses the revenue from sales to grow. Certainly, it's easier and faster to grow when you have cash to pump into your start-up, but with discipline and persistence, you can be a "rags to riches" eBay success story.

Your start-up money needs to cover your inventory, equipment, supplies, and working capital. Inventory includes the items you're going to sell. Equipment includes your computer, printer, digital camera, scanner, telephone, scales, and other equipment you need to operate. Supplies are things such as paper, labels, boxes, packing material, tape, and even small items like sticky notes and staples. Most of these items are relatively inexpensive, but they can add up. Your working capital is the money you need to operate and pay salaries while you're waiting for your business to become profitable.

If you are starting a part-time business while holding down a full-time job, your need for working capital is reduced. Just keep in mind that selling on eBay is no different than any other business in that you'll get out of it what you put into it. So, if you're only working on your eBay business a couple of hours a day, your revenue and growth will be proportionate. Of course, the smarter and more efficient you are, and the better you plan, the faster your growth will be—regardless of the number of hours you invest.

Use the process of writing your business plan to calculate how much you need to start your ideal business, then figure out how much you have. If you have all the cash you need, you're very fortunate. If you don't, you need to figure out where you can get the money or start playing with the numbers and deciding what you can do without.

To figure out what you need to get your business up and running, think about every known expense you're going to have, then add 20 percent for the unexpected. Your initial cash requirement projection should be enough to cover whatever period of time you expect to operate before you begin seeing enough income to cover your expenses. This could be a few months or longer. Be realistic in setting your income projections. Use the following categories as a guide for figuring out your start-up cash needs.

Estimated Monthly Expenses

Your ongoing monthly expenses should include the following categories.

OWNER'S SALARY

If you're going to be working full-time in your company, you should pay yourself a reasonable wage. Of course, you may opt to not take a salary in the beginning if you have other income, but start paying yourself as soon as you can.

OTHER SALARIES AND WAGES

Calculate the number of people you expect to employ, the hours they will work, and their pay rates and other compensation.

RENT OR MORTGAGE

This figure is based on how much space you need to open your business, how much space you will need as your operation grows, the type of facility (homebased, retail, office, or warehouse), and its location. If you expect substantial growth requiring more space within the first two years, consider starting with more space than you need to avoid having to move soon. If you are leasing a facility, try to negotiate a rent concession to reduce your early cash needs.

ADVERTISING

Creating marketing awareness is critical for a new business, so don't make the mistake of skimping on advertising and promotion.

SUPPLIES

Calculate all the consumable supplies you will need, such as pens, markers, labels, tape, staples, paper clips, printer supplies, and anything else you may need on a day-to-day basis.

TELEPHONE

Include your basic local service, internet access (DSL, cable, dial-up, etc.), and long distance charges.

UTILITIES

Services such as gas, electric, and water should be fairly simple to calculate. If you are homebased, you're already paying these costs. If you are moving into an established facility, the leasing agent or prior tenant can provide you with historical data regarding utility expenses. If the facility is new, the utility companies serving the area should be able to assist you in estimating the expenses.

HEALTH INSURANCE

This includes the premiums for whatever coverage you purchase for yourself and your employees, and may be offset by employee contributions.

BUSINESS INSURANCE

Your business insurance requirements depend on the type of business and product, where you are located, the value of the assets to be covered, and the potential liability involved. Get proposals from at least three commercial insurers to determine how much coverage is appropriate and what it will cost.

PAYROLL TAXES AND RELATED EXPENSES

This should encompass all required employee expenses in addition to actual wages. Also include Social Security and Medicare taxes, federal and state unemployment taxes, workers' compensation insurance, and self-employment tax on your own income if you are operating as a sole proprietor.

BUSINESS TAXES

This category includes all the various ongoing business taxes, including property taxes; intangible taxes; various city, county, and state operating license fees; and any other applicable taxes.

INTEREST

This is the cost of the money you have borrowed to start and operate your business, and can only be calculated after you have determined what your other start-up cash needs are.

MAINTENANCE

The cost of repairs and maintenance will vary depending on the type and size of your facility, and whether you own or lease. As an owner, you will bear the entire expense. As a renter, certain costs may be included in the rent, others may be shared among a group of tenants, and still others may be your own responsibility.

LEGAL, ACCOUNTING, AND CONSULTING

Estimate what you will spend for ongoing legal advice, accounting services, computer consulting, and other professional services.

MISCELLANEOUS

These are the costs that don't quite fit under any other category and are often unexpected. Your allocation for these expenses can be adjusted for accuracy once you are actually in operation.

One-Time-Only Starting Costs

Nonrepeating start-up costs include the following categories.

FIXTURES AND EQUIPMENT

These are the items necessary to create a functioning operation and could include counters, shelving, cabinets, displays, lighting, signage, cash registers, computers, furniture, and any equipment necessary to operate your business. You may buy these items outright, lease, or finance them. In the latter cases, the payments need to be included in your estimated monthly expenses.

INSTALLATION OF FIXTURES AND EQUIPMENT

Calculate the cost of shipping, uncrating, and installing the items you have listed under fixtures and equipment.

DECORATING AND REMODELING

Just about every facility will require some work to make it suitable for your operation. Get two or three bids.

STARTING INVENTORY

This will likely be the largest single start-up expense you have.

UTILITIES DEPOSITS

Contact each utility company to determine its deposit requirements. Most utilities require a deposit on commercial accounts, even if you have a great payment record as a consumer.

LEGAL AND CONSULTING FEES

These are the one-time fees involved in setting up your business, including establishing your legal structure, setting up a corporation if appropriate, and setting up your books.

LICENSES AND PERMITS

You may have to pay certain one-time fees for such items as construction permits and inspections, and other required occupational licenses.

CASH ON HAND

This is the amount of cash you need on hand to operate your business from day to day. It can be calculated from your monthly expenditures.

Finding Your Start-Up Funds

Once you know how much cash you need, you can be creative in finding it. Consider some of the following sources.

YOUR OWN RESOURCES

People generally have more in the way of assets than they realize. Do a thorough inventory of what you have, including savings accounts, equity in real estate, retirement accounts, vehicles, recreation equipment, collections, and other investments. Though you may not want to risk your retirement account to fund your eBay business, you may be willing to sell your childhood coin or stamp collection that you haven't looked at in years and your own kids don't care about. If you don't want to sell your assets for cash, use them as collateral for a loan. Or auction things you already own to raise cash to invest in inventory and equipment.

Consider your own personal line of credit. Most of the equipment you'll need is available through retail stores, web sites, and from eBay sellers who accept credit cards. You may also be able to finance inventory purchases on credit cards.

Be cautious when using credit cards for business expenses—and only charge items that will contribute to revenue generation. For example, a digital camera can speed up the time it takes to launch an auction and eliminate film processing expenses, which makes it an acceptable item to charge. If you find a great deal on wholesale merchandise and your research indicates you should be able to sell those items quickly and at a reasonable profit, that would be an acceptable item to charge.

What's not an acceptable expense to put on a credit card when you don't have the income to pay it off in full at the end of the month? A new desk, when the old table you're using is working fine and you don't have customers coming into your office that you need to impress. A fancy photo backdrop when a plain sheet will do. Or a large amount of printed letterhead that will take you years to use up.

Many successful businesses both on and off eBay have been started with credit card funding. You can do it, too. Just be smart about it.

FRIENDS AND FAMILY

The next logical step after gathering your own resources is to approach friends and relatives who believe in you and want to help you succeed. Be cautious with these arrangements. No matter how close you are, present yourself professionally, put everything in writing, and be sure the individuals you approach can afford to take the risk of investing in your business. Never accept money for a business venture from anyone who can't afford to lose that money.

If you feel shy about asking someone to invest in your business or loan you money, try this approach: Tell the person you respect his business acumen and you would appreciate it if he would review your business plan and give you his thoughts. If your financial section indicates that you're looking for outside funding, you'll know from his response to your plan whether he's interested in investing. In fact, if your plan is good enough, he may be the one to bring it up and offer funding before you ask.

Remember that money rarely comes without strings. Be sure you are very clear with your investors as to what they are getting for their money and what their role with your operation will be. You may be happy to get Great Uncle Horace's money, but do you want him telling you what to buy and sell on eBay or who to hire and fire? On the other hand, Cousin Carol may be a business and financial whiz, and you'd be thrilled to have her take an active role in your company. Or no matter how smart Cousin Carol is, you still want to do things yourself. The point is: clarify *in writing* what the total agreement is before you accept any outside funding of any kind from anybody.

PARTNERS

Most operations that sell on eBay are owned by just one person or perhaps a married couple. But there are plenty of successful partnerships. Some of those partnerships existed prior to the company starting to sell on eBay; others were created for the purpose of building an eBay operation. When considering partners as a funding source, you may look for someone who has financial resources and also wants to work side by side with you in the business. Or you may find someone who has money to invest but no interest in doing the actual work. As with your friends and family, be sure to create a written partnership agreement that clearly defines your respective responsibilities and obligations.

GOVERNMENT PROGRAMS

Take advantage of the abundance of local, state, and federal programs designed to support small business. Make your first stop the U.S. Small Business Administration (www.sba.gov); then investigate various other programs that may offer funding or support. Women, minorities, and veterans should check out niche financing possibilities designed to help these groups get into business. Check with your local economic development agency to see what sort of local and state grants or low-interest loans might be available. For example, if your business is going to create jobs, you may be eligible for a grant or tax credit for each employee.

Track Your Financial Progress

To have a profitable business of any kind, you need to stay on top of the numbers. When you're paying attention, you can correct small problems before they turn into big (and costly) disasters. And when you see something that's working well, you can do more of it right away. You also need complete and current records of your income and expenses so you can meet your tax obligations promptly.

The successful eBay sellers we talked to were always on top of their finances. For example, Nona Van Deusen (eBay User ID: stylebug.com) checks her revenue daily. Payments are recorded daily in Excel® spreadsheets and carefully monitored. The entire staff gets together monthly to discuss performance and plan sales and other strategies. Other sellers have similar routines so they always know how they're doing. If you start losing money in February and don't realize it until July, you may not be able to recover—if indeed you were able to stay in business that long.

Setting Up Your Records

Tracking your financial progress begins with setting up good records—and you should do it from day one. Before you launch your business, set up a system that allows you to keep complete and detailed records on everything you spend and receive.

Sit down with a competent tax advisor to be sure you understand all your responsibilities and obligations regarding local, state, and federal taxes. If you're going to have employees, you need to understand and follow the rules regarding wages and payroll taxes. It's always easier to set up your books right from the start than to try to clean them up later on.

Your best bet is one of the popular bookkeeping programs such as QuickBooks or Peachtree. These programs are easy to learn and use, and can generate reports as often as you like. You also need to set up files for your paper records, especially receipts for business expenses and tax payments. A filing system set up by category and year will make it easy for you to find documents when you need them.

Financial Statements

Keeping good records helps generate the financial statements that tell you exactly where you stand and what you need to do next. The key financial statements you need to understand and use regularly are as follows.

PROFIT AND LOSS STATEMENT (ALSO KNOWN AS THE P&L OR THE INCOME STATEMENT) This report shows how much money your company is making or losing over a designated period (typically monthly, quarterly, or annually) by subtracting expenses from revenue to arrive at a net result. Monthly (or even weekly) P&Ls let you watch for and respond to short-term trends or identify seasonal patterns in your business.

BALANCE SHEET

This statement is essentially a financial snapshot of your business. It shows your assets, liabilities, and capital at a specific point. Balance sheets are typically generated monthly, quarterly, and when the books are closed at the end of the year.

CASH FLOW STATEMENT

It is a report summarizing the operating, investing, and financing activities of your business as they relate to the inflow and outflow of cash. As with the profit and loss statement, a cash flow statement is prepared to reflect a specific accounting period, such as monthly, quarterly, or annually. Although this sounds similar to a profit and loss statement, it's not. The issue of cash has virtually nothing to do with profitability—it's simply tracking and managing the money coming in and going out. Profitability and liquidity do not necessarily go hand-in-hand. Your cash flow statement should be your most frequently prepared and studied financial statement.

CASH FLOW FORECAST

Similar to a cash flow statement, but this forecast projects your income and expenses into the future so you can plan your operations to meet your financial needs.

Successful eBay sellers review these reports regularly, at least monthly or even more often, so they always know where they stand and can quickly respond to financial situations when necessary. Your business may be built on an exciting concept and a great product, but its lifeblood is cash. Sound cash management is essential as you move from dream to profitability.

Know Your Costs

It's important to know what it actually costs you to sell an item on eBay. Consider your listing fees, payment fees, photography expenses, and the labor involved in creating and posting the listing. Steve Mack (eBay User ID: ztradingpost) says when he first started selling on eBay, "It was neat, it was fun, but it was not profitable. There were really high costs to sell on eBay. We found out that to sell an item cost us $23." That calculation came from doing some serious cost activity analysis, figuring out how much time it took to stage and take the photograph, research the item and write the listing, put together the auction, answer e-mails from potential bidders, and handle the end-of-auction activities. With a lot of effort and work, Mack says he got that cost down to $20—still unacceptably high.

The issue was a duplication of efforts. To sell an item on eBay required repeating the same processes for the same items that were done when the merchandise was accepted by a pawnshop. So Mack developed a software product that eliminated the duplicate work. "We were able to reduce our costs from $23 to 25 cents. Know your cost to sell," Mack says. "Know what your time is worth."

Other costs you need to understand include your overhead (the cost of operating your business, including rent, utilities, and taxes, excluding labor and materials); the total cost of your inventory (including inventory carrying costs, discussed in Chapter 5); and the cost of labor (including yours).

Control Expenses

There are two ways to improve bottom-line profits: increase sales and reduce costs. Consider this: Your business generates $1 million a year in sales at a net profit margin of 10 percent. Reduce expenses by $5,000 and you have accomplished the same bottom-line result as you would had you increased sales by $50,000. Which is easier—finding $50,000 worth of new business or trimming costs by $5,000?

Always be on the lookout for ways to eliminate waste and control costs without sacrificing quality or service to your customers. Step back and look at your operation through the eyes of an efficiency expert. Consider what you can do to improve. Some tips to think about are:

- When purchasing, keep seasonal price fluctuations and availability in mind. If you have room to store without incurring additional overhead costs, you can usually get a price break by buying in bulk when prices are down and availability is high.
- Be sure the products you buy are the most appropriate and cost-effective for your needs. The least expensive is not always the best deal.
- Set up an internal system to stay on top of rebates and manufacturer promotions. It's easy to overlook rebate deadlines or to get so distracted by day-to-day operations that you miss special offers, such as end-of-year surplus sales that will let you pick up materials at substantial savings.
- Look to your suppliers for co-op promotional support. Ask if they'll contribute to an advertising campaign or agree to a price reduction if you run a special.

Taxes

Businesses are required to pay a wide range of taxes, and there are no exceptions for companies that sell on eBay. Take the time to review all of your tax liabilities with your accountant, and keep good records so that you meet all your tax requirements on time.

Income Tax

As this book is being written, Congress is promising a major tax code overhaul. Even so, no matter how the tax laws change, it's unlikely that income tax is going to be eliminated—although it may get simpler to calculate. You must report all your income from your eBay sales, no matter how insignificant. Failing to report income is a crime. Although the IRS may not have time to scrutinize every single eBay seller, a defense of "I didn't think you would catch me" isn't going to be of much value if you are caught not reporting income.

Of course, in addition to reporting all your income, you should take every single deduction to which you are legally entitled. This includes all expenses related to the operation of your business and the sale of your products. If you are home-based, you may qualify for the home office deduction, which allows you to deduct a portion of your rent, mortgage interest, household utilities and services, real estate taxes, homeowners insurance, repairs, security systems, and depreciation. If you're driving back and forth to the post office or another shipping location, you can either deduct mileage or depreciate your car and write off the actual expenses. Don't overlook expenses such as your listing fees, final value fees, PayPal fees, and other selling-related fees.

Consult with a qualified tax advisor to determine what deductions you may take.

Sales Tax

Sales tax can be a challenging issue for eBay sellers—and the biggest challenge is that laws are inconsistent from state to state. Many large retailers with online operations have begun collecting sales tax on internet sales, and legislation affecting how internet sales are taxed is pending at state and federal levels. As a business owner, you are responsible for knowing the law and doing the right thing. Whether you need to collect and remit state and local sales tax depends on a variety of factors, including your product line, where your business is located, and where your customers are. Also, many states have what's known as casual sale exemptions that might apply if you're just selling your own items in what amounts to an online garage sale.

The bottom line on sales tax is to know the rules of the state you're in. Your accountant or your state's revenue department should be able to help you understand the regulations as they apply to your specific business.

To charge and collect sales tax, you'll need a sales tax ID number (sometimes referred to as a reseller's permit). This is usually a very simple process; just check with your state's department of revenue for information on how to proceed.

When you are buying items for resale, you generally do not have to pay sales tax. Your suppliers will need to see a copy of your sales tax ID certificate. If a buyer tells you she is sales tax exempt—either because she's buying for resale or qualifies in other ways, such as a church or other nonprofit—insist on having a copy of the tax certificate before you remove the sales tax from the invoice.

Other Taxes

In addition to income and sales tax, your business may be subject to a wide range of other taxes. If you have employees, you'll be responsible for payroll taxes. If you operate as a corporation, you'll have to pay payroll taxes for yourself; as a sole proprietor, you'll pay self-employment tax. Then there are property taxes, taxes on your equipment and inventory, intangible taxes, fees and taxes to maintain your corporate status, your business license fee (which is really a tax), and other lesser-known taxes.

The penalties for failing to pay the right amount of taxes on time can be substantial, even when the reason for nonpayment was an honest mistake, so it's worth consulting with a qualified tax advisor to make sure you have everything covered.

Forecasting Revenue

Now that we've talked about how much you need to spend to have a business selling on eBay, what can you expect to make? Regular eBay sellers can generate revenue ranging from just a few dollars a month to literally millions. The challenge for new eBay sellers—as it is for any new business owner—is figuring out what your sales are likely to be when you don't have a history to use as a basis.

Study the pricing strategies discussed in Chapter 7. Next, consider how many auctions you'll be able to launch per week or month, how many items you can expect to stock in your eBay store, what your average sale will be, and what percentage of those auctions and store listings are likely to result in completed sales. Your initial revenue forecasts will probably need revising as you begin operations and see actual results.

Keep track of your average selling price (ASP). If, for example, most of your auctions close with a final value price of less than $10, you have to sell and ship a lot of items to make a decent living. Track your ASP, and look for ways to increase it. Can you add accessories? Sell in larger lots? For most eBay sellers who are getting a decent margin on their products, an ASP of $30 to $50 will give you a worthwhile return.

Funding Growth

If you thought finding start-up capital was a challenge, here's some news you may not be happy to know: Getting the money to fund growth can be more difficult than start-up funds. For eBay sellers, that's typically because start-up needs are modest but growth needs are more substantial.

For example, Van Deusen purchased her initial inventory using her personal credit cards. "Then I started buying huge quantities of merchandise, so I had to get a loan almost to triple digits," she says. "It was difficult." Fortunately, she was able to borrow from her family as well as from a bank, which made the process a little easier.

It's a good idea to think about your expansion funding long before you need it. Establish a credit line with your bank so money will be available when an opportunity arises. Expect lenders to be cautious about approving a loan—especially if they don't know much about the strength and power of eBay. As you did when you approached funding sources for your start-up capital, be professional, polished, and prepared. Be able to show clear financial statements demonstrating your solid history and growth potential, and be prepared to sign a personal guarantee for the loan or to put up your business assets as collateral.

Profitability Is the Measure of Business Success

You can calculate the profitability of your eBay operation by using the free profit calculator at www.nortica.com. From the home page, click on "User Area," then on "Profit Calculator," and follow the instructions.

The key to profitability on eBay is efficiency. If you can create an efficient system, you can plug any product into it and make money. If you are not consistently and regularly profitable, you are not running an eBay business—you're running an eBay hobby.

CHAPTER 16

Human Resources: Staffing Your eBay Operation

LENTY OF EBAY SELLERS EITHER WORK alone or in casual operations with family members. But the high-volume sellers have employees—and it just makes sense. Think about what it takes to send out hundreds of packages a week. One person just can't do it all.

If starting a business is like giving birth—exciting, frightening, painful, exhilarating—then hiring your first employee may well be compared to choosing your child's first babysitter. It's a decision that is critical to the overall health, well-being, and future of your company—and it can be a traumatic experience.

Hiring deserves as much research and planning as developing your concept, deciding what to sell, and structuring your operation. And your first employee will set the tone for all the hiring you do in the future.

Ideally, that first employee should provide a balance to your own strengths and weaknesses—definitely an easier-said-than-done type of task. It's much easier to hire someone who is like yourself because you're comfortable with her. Though personal compatibility is certainly important, your first priority should be to meet the needs of your business. If you're building a company, you need a broad range of skills—skills that are different when you're building an eBay company than for a brick-and-mortar operation.

Out-of-the-Ordinary Workers

What's different about the employees you hire for an eBay operation? "Computer skills is the biggest thing," says Michael Jansma (eBay User ID: gemaffair). He explains that if you are hiring someone for a brick-and-mortar retail sales position, you would want them to make a good appearance and know how to close a sale. "But if I'm hiring somebody for my sales floor [which is eBay], it's totally different. They need to have some sales experience, but they don't need to know anything about a close. They don't need to know how to dress. They don't really need to know a lot about seasonality or trends, or up-selling, or any of that stuff. They need to have some computer knowledge." They also need to be able to communicate clearly via e-mail and to write auction listings that evoke an emotional response, he adds.

"Selling on eBay is like a team sport. You have a certain person who does a job and the next person picks it up, and we are all working together," says Nona Van Deusen (eBay User ID: stylebug.com). "They are not the typical kind of employees, I think. They are more open to a different kind of working atmosphere; not one that you would picture in a corporate office. We all dress comfortably coming to work. I even used to bring my dog to work before customers started coming in. It was real laid back." Laid back, yes. But still hard working.

Always keep in mind that hiring mistakes can be expensive, both from an economic perspective as well as damage to your company. So do your homework.

The First Step in Hiring

Before reading the first resume or accepting any applications, have your hiring system in place. Read some books and articles on employee selection and hiring, and then work out a process that makes sense to you and is compatible with the company you want to build.

You don't need to become an expert on labor law, but you do need to know enough to avoid asking illegal questions or committing other missteps that could leave you open to civil liability. At the same time, you need to be able to gather as much information as possible about the candidates you're considering in order to make the best choice. Some tips for developing your hiring procedures include the following.

Write a Job Description

Job descriptions don't have to be literary masterpieces, but they do need to clearly outline the duties and responsibilities of the position, and the skills required for adequate performance. For example, if the job requires knowledge of certain equipment or particular software, be specific about it in the job description. But don't demand more than you actually require. If you want someone to handle your packing and shipping and the job requires just enough computer savvy to be able to print labels and enter status reports, don't insist on the ability to type 60 words per minute. A slower speed is probably sufficient. Focus instead on determining if your candidate is conscientious, pays attention to detail, and will make sure the right merchandise is shipped.

Establish a Salary Range and Benefits Package

It's a good idea to put this in writing and provide it to candidates during the interview. In a tight labor market, you have to sell your company to candidates as hard as they have to sell themselves to you.

Have a Job Application Form

Every prospective employee should complete an application form, even if she has submitted a detailed resume. A resume is not a signed, sworn statement affirming that the information contained is the truth and that you can fire the individual if she lies; the application is. Asking for an application will also help you verify the information on resumes. Check it for consistency. You can develop your own application or purchase blank forms at an office supply store. In either case, have an attorney review your form before using it to make sure you are not asking any illegal questions.

Prepare Your Interview Questions in Advance

Make them appropriate to the job, of course, but ask each candidate the same set of questions. Take notes as they respond so you can make an accurate assessment and comparison later.

Develop Open-Ended Questions that Encourage a Candidate to Talk

In addition to knowing what experience each candidate has had, you want to find out more of the details. Ask for descriptions and explanations. Ask a candidate to tell you about the worst thing that ever happened on the job or the most difficult customer he had to handle and what he did. Give him a hypothetical situation that he might encounter on the job with you, and ask how he'd handle it.

Be Sparing with How Much Information You Provide Up Front

If you tell a candidate what you want, a smart one will just feed that back to you. Of course, you have an obligation to tell a candidate about your company and what you're looking for so she can decide whether she wants to work for you. It's a two-way process—but let her do the talking first.

When your procedures are in place, you can start looking. Be creative; don't just place a "help wanted" ad in your local paper. Network with personal and professional associates to identify prospective employees. Check with nearby colleges and perhaps even high schools for part-time help. Consider using a temporary help or employment agency. Put the word out among your social contacts as well—you never know who might have a connection to the perfect person for your company. However, use caution if you decide to hire friends or relatives. Many personal relationships have not been strong enough to survive an employee-employer situation.

Getting through the Interview

Especially when you first start hiring, expect to be as nervous about the interview process as the candidates. This person may need a job, but you need the right person on your staff. Think of the employment relationship as a marriage that happens after a very brief courtship. You might spend a few hours in two or three different interviews with the person, a little more time checking references, and then you make a decision that could result in a multi-year or even multi-decade relationship. That's why the interview process is so critical.

In the first interview, focus on whether the candidate has the qualifications you need. If he doesn't, neither one of you needs to waste any more time. During your second meeting, tell him more about your company and what you expect, and gauge his reaction. Assuming that meeting goes well, get together one more time before you make an offer. If possible, the third interview should be in a more casual setting, perhaps over breakfast or lunch. You'll see a side of him you might not see in a traditional interview environment. If he's rude to a server in a restaurant, he'll likely be rude to co-workers he considers subordinate.

When each interview is over, let candidates know what to expect. Explain the next step in your hiring process—another interview, a background check, whatever—and be definitive on when they will hear from you.

Be sure to document every step of the interview and reference-checking process. Even very small companies are finding themselves the targets of employment discrimination suits; good records are your best defense if it happens to you.

Making the Choice

Take the same approach to quality with your employees as you do with your product. If you wouldn't sell substandard merchandise to your customers, don't hire someone with substandard skills to serve them. Though you may be tempted to cut financial corners with payroll, it's a penny-wise, pound-foolish strategy. If the person who works for $20 a week less in salary makes mistakes that cost you thousands of dollars, you don't have a bargain—you have a liability. Invest in someone who has the skills and abilities you need and who can help you grow your company. It's also important not to over-hire. Hire what you need, or perhaps one step up, but don't hire today what you're going to need in ten years because that person is going to become discontented and leave. In other words, don't hire a topnotch manager for a customer service rep job.

As much as possible, try to give the applicant a taste of the job before either of you make a commitment. Invite a candidate to spend time watching your operation. Consider a trial period or other mutual evaluation method. Ask someone who will be writing auction descriptions and answering e-mails to give you a sample of her work. Once you have employees on board, allow them to interact with candidates during the hiring process and give you feedback on their impressions.

Decision Made—Now What?

The hiring process doesn't end with making the selection. Your new employee's first day is critical. Get prepared for him. Welcome him into the company, have a place set up to work, and make him comfortable. Take the time to adequately train him, and don't assume he knows how you operate or what you want if you haven't told him.

Incentives Work

Give everyone on your staff a reason to go the extra mile by rewarding excellent performance. "I have an incentive program," Van Deusen says. "If we reach certain goals, everyone gets a bonus check every month, and that is an encouragment to write better listings and take better photographs. It includes everyone in the whole process. We have five levels of bonuses based on our net sales at the end of the month. Whatever level we reach, the bonus goes up from there. Then we also do individual bonuses if I think an employee really went above and beyond."

You may offer a commission on sales or extra cash for other measurable results. Be sure your incentive program is truly an incentive program. Bonuses must be based on clearly-defined goals that take work to achieve. When people get bonuses for no real reason, two things happen. First, the "bonuses" become entitlements; workers expect them and feel ripped off if they don't get them. Second, when there's no real reward for superior performance, it's human nature to not stretch beyond average.

Maintain Complete Personnel Files

An important part of administering your business includes maintaining complete and current personnel files. Store these documents in a secure place, such as a locked filing cabinet, and limit who has access to them.

Personnel files are used to make job-related decisions affecting employees and therefore should contain only information that can be legally used in making those decisions. Because federal and state law prohibits the use of sex, race, national origin, color, religion, disability, or veteran's status to make employment decisions, documents containing this information should not be included in personnel files. Similarly, medical information, garnishment orders and records, and I-9 documents should be filed separately from the employee's primary personnel file.

The information you need to maintain on each employee includes

- the signed and dated employment application, resume, and other hiring records.
- basic employee information: name, address, Social Security number, date of birth, job classification, I-9, and work permits for minors.
- a copy of your offer of employment.
- all employment actions, including hires, separations, rehires, promotions, demotions, transfers, layoffs, and recalls.
- a current photo of the employee that you update annually. This does not need to be a portrait; a snapshot taken with an instant or digital camera is sufficient.
- copies of any pre-employment testing, including drug test results.
- copies of all special qualifications, including licenses and certifications.
- records of any training the employee completes after coming on board.
- copies of performance reviews, commendations, and discipline or other corrective action notices.
- payroll information.
- records of any job-related illnesses and injuries.
- home address, telephone number, and emergency contact information.
- a copy of current, valid driver's license for employees who drive as part of their job and a copy of current insurance certificate for employees who use their own vehicle on the job.

Employees Are Essential

If your goal is a high-volume business, you're going to need employees—and that may be one of the biggest challenges of running your company. In fact, most entrepreneurs say that finding and keeping good employees is one of the hardest things to do. But if you're going to grow, you have to do it.

eBay Potpourri: Ideas and Advice You Can Use Now

OUR GOAL WAS TO PUT TOGETHER AN organized book that would take you step by step through the process of starting and operating a successful, profitable business selling on eBay. We've told you how to get set up, sell your items, run your company, hire people, manage the financial side of your operation, and more. After all that, we still have information that just didn't fit in any of the preceding chapters. So here it is: ideas, advice, and resources for your eBay operation that you can begin using right now.

Stay Informed

To stay current with auction market news, events, and information, subscribe to online auction newsletters and participate in discussion forums. Interacting with a newsgroup provides support and promotes learning and collaboration, whether you are the student or the mentor. Find a couple of discussion groups in your area of interest and contribute regularly by asking questions and offering advice. Some of the most popular auction-related discussion groups are on eBay, Yahoo!, Topica, AOL, and MSN. Just visit the sites and search under "eBay auctions."

"I suggest that anyone who is starting out on eBay find at least one of these groups," says Maggie Donapel (eBay User ID: plumsbooks). "You can ask all of your questions and get a lot of answers." Donapel and Georgene Harkness (eBay User ID: mynewthreads) also recommend AuctionBytes.com as a great informational site that offers discussion forums for sellers as well as valuable articles and newsletters.

Discussion boards and forums can also be effective vehicles for networking. When posting, include your full signature line (if allowed by the moderator) so others know who you are and what you do. But be discreet—many groups have strict rules about blatant self-promotion.

If you want to specifically promote your listings, there are newsgroups exclusively for posting and advertising auctions. Others allow auction ads on certain days of the week, and still others prohibit promoting auctions completely. When you join a group, find out what the rules are and don't violate them. Mind your manners, and don't spam list members with auction announcements.

Kathy Logan (eBay User ID: rosie_peachstate) belongs to more than 80 Yahoo! groups and says that's where much of her sales come from. She is only active on a few of the lists, but scans the others for posts that she might reply to in a way that will help someone else and also promote her business. "Only two groups are associated with eBay specifically," she says. "The rest are related to my business, which is arts and crafts. Whenever I post on these groups with my signature link, it's like using a billboard on the interstate." Except that it's free, more targeted, and probably produces better results.

Stay Active in the eBay Community

eBay is constantly updating and revising its policies, features, web site, and fee structures. As a seller you have a responsibility to stay informed about these changes, as they could impact your business and how you operate. Participating in the eBay community also allows you to share your expertise while giving your business more exposure.

Though literally billions of dollars in sales have been transacted on eBay, the sales venue is far from mature. "Everyone is still learning, trying to figure it out," says Steve Mack (eBay User ID: ztradingpost). And they're working together so that everybody learns.

Start by clicking on the "Community" link that is available on any eBay page. From there you can access discussion boards, find answers to questions and discuss problems with fellow sellers, participate in workshops and other eBay events, read special announcements, and sign up for newsletter notifications.

Community Discussion Boards

This is a great place to find help with specific concerns such as feedback, checkout policies, international trading, and tools. You can also talk with other sellers about category specific issues like sports, antiques, books, or computers. There are general discussion boards for newbies, old-timers, night owls, sharing great ideas, or grousing about pet peeves. There are also question and answer boards for when you are trying to find the solution to a problem as quickly as possible or want to offer advice to a fellow eBayer.

eBay Groups Center

At the Groups Center you can hook up with fellow eBayers who have common interests, such as collectibles, education, and families. You may want to find folks who are in your town or region. Several mentoring groups are available to teach you eBay basics, such as selling, writing a listing, hosting photographs, setting up a store, or balancing a full-time job with your eBay business. One of the eBay groups that Gary Neubert (eBay User ID: gatorpack) participates in is the Professional Sellers eBay Alliance. This group is in the process of being incorporated as a not-for-profit trade association and is made up of more than 600 Power Sellers that are at a Titanium or Platinum level.

eBay News Center

Here you can sign up to receive special announcements about eBay policies, features, programs, and systems, as well as notifications about eBay's monthly newsletter. This is definitely an area you want to plug into.

eBay Calendar and Events

Watch the calendar and look at the events list for dates on upcoming workshops, trade shows, community events and more. There are several events each month that provide great networking opportunities. These events are both virtual and real world, allowing you to connect and learn through the format you're most comfortable with.

eBay Help Section

eBay features an extensive Help section that includes tutorials and workshops to help familiarize you with buying and selling practices. Harkness said she spent a lot of time reading this section when she first started on eBay. "The Help files are actually pretty good on eBay," she says. "They are very instructive, so I just stayed with it until I felt comfortable enough to start selling a couple of things." While the content is complete and easy to understand, you may be occasionally challenged when you try to find specific information. Keep searching—sometimes you have to phrase your search request a little differently to get what you need.

Outside the Online World

In addition to receiving news updates and participating in discussion forums, join a real-world professional or trade association related to your field or online auctions in general. Your membership is a demonstration of your commitment to quality and excellence in your business. Be sure to mention your affiliations on your About Me page or in your signature line.

Get Professional Help When You Need It

No one can be an expert about everything. Call on professionals—attorneys, accountants, tax advisors—when you need them.

A critical need for most eBay sellers is a computer consultant. After all, if your computers go down, you're essentially out of business until you get them back up and running. Choose your computer consultant and web designer carefully. "They can put a real dent in your budget," Van Deusen says. "A lot of consultants claim to know more than they do, and I've learned the hard way. It's so difficult to find a good one." Van Deusen finally took a class on web design and took over that aspect of her operation. Learn enough about computers and the internet so you can at least evaluate what the experts are telling you.

Have a Disaster Plan

When a blizzard was approaching Ohio last winter, one eBay seller added this line to his automatic winning notification e-mails: "We normally ship within 24 hours of receiving payment. However, we are preparing for a severe winter storm and may be without power when this auction ends. If that is the case, we will ship your merchandise and update our computers as soon as possible after power is restored. Thank you for your patience and understanding."

A key part of coping with a disaster is communicating with your customers so they know what to expect. You should also have a plan to communicate with your suppliers so they don't try to make a delivery if you're not open. And, of course, you need a system that backs up all of your electronic data in an off-site location. The Red Cross and your local emergency management agency can help you with the details of putting together a disaster plan for your operation.

Don't Be a Victim of a Scam

Though eBay is an open, trusting community, it's not immune to thieves who will try to steal information in order to steal cash or merchandise. Con artists typically infiltrate users' accounts through common e-mail scams that are deviously made up to look like official notices from eBay or PayPal. These messages advise recipients to confirm their IDs, passwords, or other sensitive information by sending them to a web site that snags the information and turns the unknowing user into a victim of identity theft. These scams are called "spoofing" or "phishing." While some are obvious frauds, others appear to be quite legitimate, such as one that pops in as a PayPal payment that is bogus. The bottom line is to never, ever give out personal information that is requested via e-mail. Always forward these types of e-mails to spoof@ebay.com or spoof@paypal.com for verification. eBay and PayPal will immediately follow up on it. If you are concerned that the e-mail may be legitimate and you need to take some action with an account, never use the link in the e-mail. Instead, close the e-mail, and access your account through the company's main web site.

Logan discovered she had been the victim of eBay identity theft when she logged onto her account one morning and saw a 52-inch plasma TV for $2,600 mixed in her arts and crafts listings. "In my little Pollyanna world I don't think anybody ever hurts anybody else, so I just assumed eBay had a glitch that would take care of itself," she says. "But later that day an eBay representative called me to say they noticed something in my listings that I don't normally sell. I said, 'Yeah, it's a TV. Do you want to buy it?' The woman laughed and then told me they thought my account had been compromised."

As it turned out, an overseas hacker had obtained access to Logan's User ID and password and had rerouted e-mails to his address so he could answer any questions about the bogus listing. The hacker had also set up an elaborate wire transfer scheme so the money could not be traced. Within a couple of hours eBay was able to bring everything to a screeching halt before the transaction closed and money was exchanged. "I was really impressed with eBay's whole performance in that scenario," Logan says.

Monitor your eBay and PayPal accounts carefully, and take immediate action when something doesn't look right. To stay current on the latest online scams and frauds, visit Internet Scambusters at www.scambusters.org and subscribe to their free newsletter.

Mediocre Isn't Good Enough

Make everything you do on eBay your absolute best. Don't post a fuzzy picture and think it's OK—it's not. Don't get careless with a description and figure the item will still sell—it might, but probably for less that you could have gotten. Don't shortchange your descriptions—eBay doesn't charge per word, so give the prospective buyer a good visual using descriptive words.

Don't do anything halfway or just "good enough." As a buyer, you want the best from sellers. As a seller, don't offer your customers anything less.

Pay Attention

Always know exactly what you're selling. Harkness learned that the hard way when she hurriedly posted a few items she had found at a dollar store. "I didn't look at them very closely before listing them. One was a figurine of two frogs on an island. Shortly after putting it on eBay I received a message from someone asking if it wouldn't be more appropriate to put that auction in the Mature Audience category," she says. "This was before I had quit my day job, so I immediately called my husband from work and told him to go look at that thing and tell me what it was." As it turns out, the figurine was of a male frog standing behind a female frog with his "hands" in inappropriate places—something Harkness hadn't noticed. "I guess you could say that one of my first learning experiences as a seller on eBay was, 'Look closely at what you are selling,'" she says.

Give Your eBay Business an Annual Checkup

You go to the doctor and dentist every year for a checkup. You have the air conditioner in your house checked every spring and the heater checked in the winter—why not do the same thing for your business operation? Are you taking advantage of all the new features eBay routinely introduces? Are you promoting your auctions, your store, and your overall business to the best advantage? "I never feel satisfied with what we are doing," Van Deusen says. "I am always trying to improve it."

Schedule a time every year to give your business a thorough checkup. Get out your business plan and compare what you said you were going to do with what you actually did. If there was a variance, figure out why. Review all of your procedures and systems to be sure you are operating as efficiently and profitably as possible. And browse through eBay's site as though you were brand new, looking for new features and services you can use.

Know that the Only Constant Is Change

Just as the brick-and-mortar world is not static, neither is eBay. You need to be able to manage the impact of economic cycles, respond to changes in pricing and demand, and adjust your business based on the marketplace. Stay flexible, pay attention to trends, and make changes in your operation when necessary.

You are operating in what might well be the world's most exciting and innovative sales venue. The eBay of tomorrow is going to be bigger and better than it is today. Congratulations on having the vision to understand that—and to take action on it.

In Chapter 1, we referred to the "wonderful world of eBay." Welcome to that world!

Internet Resource Directory for eBay Sellers

eBay Sites of Interest

eBay Affiliate Program (http://affiliates.ebay.com/). Make money on eBay without selling a thing.

eBay Business Marketplace (www.ebaybusiness.com). For the small business owner.

eBay Help (http://pages.ebay.com/help/index.html). Find the answers to all of your eBay questions here.

eBay Keywords (www.ebaykeywords.com) or (www.admarketplace.net). Find out how to increase your sales using keywords.

Seller Central (http://pages.ebay.com/sellercentral/). The best place to go for the latest tips, tools, information, and resources for selling on eBay.

What's Hot at eBay's Seller Central (http://pages.ebay.com/sellercentral/what shot.html). Find out the latest promotions, items, and trends on eBay.

eBay Subsidiaries

Elance Online (www.elance.com). Outsourcing solution for freelancers and clients.

Half.com (www.half.com). Sell selected items at a fixed price.

PayLoadz (www.payloadz.com). Not a subsidiary, but interfaces very well with eBay and PayPal for digitally downloadable products.

PayPal (www.paypal.com). Online payment system and auction management services.

Online Payment Systems

BidPay (www.bidpay.com). Free for sellers; buyers pay a fee. Used most frequently to send money orders, especially by international buyers.

Escrow.com (www.escrow.com). Escrow service used by eBay; accepts payments by credit cards, PayPal, checks, wire transfers, money orders, and cashier's checks.

PayPal (www.paypal.com). Subsidiary of eBay. Free for buyers; sellers pay a percentage fee.

Government Sites and Selling Internationally

Federal Government Official Web Site (www.firstgov.gov/shopping/auctions/auctions.shtml). Information about federal and state government auctions.

International Trading Center on eBay (http://pages.ebay.com/internationaltrading/). Tips and tools for eBayers who want to buy and sell outside of the United States.

U.S. Customs and Border Protection (www.cbp.gov). Information about importing and exporting.

U.S. Department of State (www.state.gov). Good site to visit when shopping for overseas suppliers and/or to find out information on different countries. Also has links to web sites of U.S. embassies and consulates around the world.

U.S. Small Business Administration (www.sba.gov). Information and support for small businesses.

U.S. Treasury Department (www.treasury.gov/auctions/). Information about government auctions.

Auction Management Tools

All My Auctions (www.rajeware.com). This tracks your auctions; compiles reports; has an auction calculator, templates for e-mails, shipping labels, and packing slips.

Andale (www.andale.com). Has many auction tools including research, store, and management, including free counters.

Auction Submit Software (www.auctionsubmit.com). Free software for submitting auctions to multiple sites and other auction management functions. Has additional software programs available for a fee.

Market Works (www.auctionworks.com). Comprehensive list of auction tools and services.

Nortica 100 (www.nortica.com). To find out the top 100 eBay sellers based on feedback ratings and transaction amounts, click "User Area." This site also features several product downloads (most with a free trial) to help manage and improve your eBay auctions.

Shooting Star (www.foodogsoftware.com). Manages and tracks all of your auctions and lets you know what you need to do when.

The Poster Toaster (www.thepostertoaster.com). Free bulk listing tool.

ViewTracker™ (www.sellathon.com). Tracking software that tells you how auction visitors found you, keywords searched, categories browsed, how search results were sorted, if people watched your auction, planned a snipe, and more.

Free Auction Templates

Auction Moms (www.auctionmoms.com). Good for beginners; also offers other tools, tips, and resources.

Auction Riches (www.auctionriches.com). Free basic ad creator with simple colored borders and backgrounds. Also offers many others services for a fee.

Auction Supplies (www.auctionsupplies.com). Interesting templates for people who have some experience with HTML.

Nucite (www.nucite.com). Limited selection of free templates, but great quality. Many other templates and services are available for a fee.

Miscellaneous Tools

Froogle (www.froogle.com). A shopping tool that can help you find out what specific items are selling for on the internet.

JPEG Magic (www.jpegmagic.com). Image optimizer and compressor tool with an easy interface for rotating, lightening, and darkening photos.

Speed Typing (www.colorpilot.com). Free program that allows you to store frequently used phrases and paragraphs so you can drop them into e-mails or auction descriptions.

Thank You Notes (www.ethical2004.com). A tool available through Ethical Technologies that will send every bidder note thanking them for bidding.

Auction Sniping Programs

AuctionBlitz (www.auctionblitz.com)

AuctionSniper (www.auctionsniper.com)

eSnipe (www.esnipe.com)

PowerSnipe (www.powersnipe.com)

Online Shipping and Postage Resources

Endicia Internet Postage (www.endicia.com)

FedEx (www.fedex.com)

Stamps.com (www.stamps.com)

United Parcel Service, UPS (www.ups.com)

United States Postal Service, USPS (www.usps.gov)

Photo Hosting

AuctionPix (www.auctionpix.com). Offers two options, pay per image or for designated space.

FTP Voyager (www.ftpvoyager.com). FTP software to upload pictures.

HostPCI (www.hostpci.com). Economical photo hosting service for medium-to-high volume sellers.

PhotoBucket (www.photobucket.com). Free photo hosting service.

WS_FTP (www.ipswitch.com). FTP software to upload pictures.

Web Site Domain Registration, Hosting, Development

Direct Marketing Association (www.the-dma.org/privacy/creating.shtml). Free privacy policy generator.

GoDaddy (www.godaddy.com). Economical web hosting and domain name registration.

Nameboy (www.nameboy.com). Domain name search; makes suggestions on other name availability; can register your domain name.

NetFirms (www.netfirms.com). Reasonable packages for web hosting, domain registration, e-mail, and web design tools.

Web Dev Tips (www.webdevtips.com/webdevtips/codegen/privacy.shtml). Free privacy policy generator.

Autoresponder Services for Newsletters and Announcements

Aweber (www.aweber.com)

Constant Contact (www.constantcontact.com)

Topica (http://topica.com/)

Yahoo! Groups (http://groups.yahoo.com/)

Gift Certificate Templates

KoolPrint (www.koolprint.com)

Microsoft Office Online (www.office.microsoft.com)

Trade Show Information

Tradeshow News Network (www.tsnn.com)

Tradeshow Week Online (www.tradeshowweek.com)

Popular Internet Searches

Ask Jeeves IQ Interesting Queries (http://sp.ask.com/docs/about/jeevesiq.html). Provides a weekly recap of the most popular search terms.

Lycos 50 Daily Report (http://50.lycos.com/). Features the top 50 keyword searches conducted on Lycos the previous week. The "Greatest Hits" section includes articles and predictions on trends.

Webmaster Toolkit—Keyword Research Tool (http://www.webmaster-toolkit.com/keyword-research-tool.shtml). Helps you research words and phrases while specifying a search engine of your choice.

Wordtracker (www.wordtracker.com). Online ticker featuring the top 50 items searched for in the past 24 hours. Also has a free keyword weekly report with 500 of the most frequently searched keywords.

Yahoo Buzz Index (http://buzz.yahoo.com/). Find out what Yahoo users are searching for, plus see articles on trends and hot topics.

Miscellaneous

Internet Scambusters (www.scambusters.org). Stay current on the latest online scams and frauds.

Glossary

Affiliate programs. Agreements that allow someone to endorse a product or service through web site links and receive a commission when a purchase is made.

Bid cancellation. The cancellation of a bid by a buyer or seller.

Bid increment. The amount by which a bid is increased each time the current bid is outdone.

Bid retraction. Withdrawing a bid; bid retractions are rarely allowed on eBay.

Bid shielding. Using secondary user IDs or other eBay members to temporarily raise the level of bidding to extremely high levels in order to protect the low bid level of another bidder; when bid shielding, the high bidder retracts the bid before the auction closes.

Blocked bidder list. A list of eBay users who are blocked from bidding on another user's auctions.

Cause marketing. Doing good works while promoting a for-profit product or service.

Completed search. A search of eBay auctions that have ended.

Digitally downloadable products. Digital items such as music, software, videos, and e-books that can be purchased online and immediately downloaded to the buyer's computer.

Drop-ship. When merchandise is shipped from a location other than your own to your customer as though you were shipping it.

Dutch auction. When the seller has two or more identical items offered in the same auction; also known as a Multiple Item Auction.

eBay toolbar. A collection of tools primary used by bidders that sits on your desktop as a single block of buttons.

Export license. A document indicating that a government has granted a licensee the right to export specified goods to specified countries.

Feedback. Comments made by one user about another regarding the trading experience between the two.

Final value. The final bid on an auction; the amount for which the item sells.

Final value fee. The percentage of the final value that is paid to eBay as part of the listing fees.

HTML. Stands for Hyper Text Markup Language, a simple language used to create web pages that can also be used to enhance eBay listings.

Insertion fee. The nonrefundable fee charged by eBay to post a listing; fees vary by type of listing.

Landing page. The entry point on a web site a visitor reaches from an inbound link.

Minimum bid. The lowest amount that can be entered as a bid for a specific auction.

Non-paying bidder. A bidder who wins auctions but then does not pay; eBay has strict policies for dealing with non-paying bidders.

Opening value. Another term for starting price or minimum bid.

Outbid. When another buyer has placed a higher maximum bid than the current highest bidder.

Power Seller. eBay's most successful sellers that operate in accordance with stringent requirements.

Private auction. On eBay, a type of auction where the bidders' e-mail addresses are not disclosed on the item screen or the bidding history screen.

Proxy bidding. A service that allows you to enter the maximum amount you're willing to pay for an item, then the eBay system automatically places bids on your behalf, increasing your bid as necessary by the standard increments to maintain your high bid position.

Reserve price. A hidden minimum amount the seller is willing to accept for an item listed for auction.

Reserve price auction. An auction that has a reserve price; buyers are not shown the reserve price, and sellers are not obligated to sell if the reserve price is not met.

Return Merchandise Authorization (RMA). Usually a code number issued by a seller who agrees to accept a return.

Second chance offer. Offering a nonwinning bidder a chance to purchase your item.

Shadowing. Watching other bidders to see what they're buying and how much they're paying.

Shill bidding. The deliberate placing of bids to artificially raise the price of an item; shill bidding is not allowed on eBay and is illegal in many jurisdictions.

Shilling. An old auction term that means using phony bids to inflate prices.

Spam. Unsolicited commercial e-mail.

Starting price. The price at which bidding on your auction begins; also, the lowest price you are willing to accept unless you have specified a reserve price.

Trading Assistant. An experienced eBay seller who sells items on eBay for other people.

Trading Post. A store or other type of drop-off location operated by a highly experienced Trading Assistant.

User ID. The name by which you are known on eBay.

Wholesale. The sale of goods in large quantities, usually for resale.

Index